Collins

KS3
History
Workbook

Alf Wilkinson

Revision Tips

Rethink Revision

Have you ever taken part in a quiz and thought '*I know this!*', but no matter how hard you scrabbled around in your brain you just couldn't come up with the answer?

It's very frustrating when this happens, but in a fun situation it doesn't really matter. However, in tests and assessments, it is essential that you can recall the relevant information when you need to.

Most students think that revision is about making sure you **know** *stuff*, but it is also about being confident that you can **retain** that *stuff* over time and **recall** it when needed.

Revision that Really Works

Experts have found that there are two techniques that help with *all* of these things and consistently produce better results in tests and exams compared to other revision techniques.

Applying these techniques to your KS3 revision will ensure you get better results in tests and assessments and will have all the relevant knowledge at your fingertips when you start studying for your GCSEs.

It really isn't rocket science either – you simply need to:
- **test yourself** on each topic as many times as possible
- **leave a gap** between the test sessions.

It is most effective if you leave a good period of time between the test sessions, e.g. between a week and a month. The idea is that just as you start to forget the information, you force yourself to recall it again, keeping it fresh in your mind.

Three Essential Revision Tips

1 Use Your Time Wisely
- Allow yourself plenty of time
- Try to start revising six months before tests and assessments – it's more effective and less stressful
- Your revision time is precious so use it wisely – using the techniques described on this page will ensure you revise effectively and efficiently and get the best results
- Don't waste time re-reading the same information over and over again – it's time-consuming and not effective!

2 Make a Plan
- Identify all the topics you need to revise (this Workbook will help you)
- Plan at least five sessions for each topic
- A one-hour session should be ample to test yourself on the key ideas for a topic
- Spread out the practice sessions for each topic – the optimum time to leave between each session is about one month but, if this isn't possible, just make the gaps as big as realistically possible.

3 Test Yourself
- Methods for testing yourself include: quizzes, practice questions, flashcards, past-papers, explaining a topic to someone else, etc.
- This Workbook gives you opportunities to check your progress
- Don't worry if you get an answer wrong – provided you check what the right answer is, you are more likely to get the same or similar questions right in future!

Visit our website to download your free flashcards, for more information about the benefits of these revision techniques and for further guidance on how to plan ahead and make them work for you.

collins.co.uk/collinsks3revision

Contents

Britain 1066–1509

The Norman Conquest

1 1066 was the year of three kings. Which three kings ruled England in 1066?

....

....

.... **[3]**

2 Which of these kings had, in your opinion, the strongest claim to the throne?

....

....

....

.... **[5]**

3 Where was the deciding battle in October 1066?

.... **[1]**

4 Who won this battle, and was crowned King on Christmas Day 1066?

.... **[1]**

5 What did William carry out in 1085 to find out who owned all the land in England?

.... **[1]**

6 Give **three** reasons historians think that William ordered his servants to carry out the survey.

....

....

....

....

....

.... **[3]**

7 The Bayeux Tapestry below was made in Normandy, 10 years after the Battle of Hastings. It shows the story of William from invasion to coronation. It was probably commissioned by Bishop Odo, who was William's half-brother.

How useful is the tapestry as evidence of the events leading up to William becoming King of England?

....

....

....

....

....

....

.... [5]

8 Read Source A and then answer the question that follows.

Source A: From the *Anglo-Saxon Chronicle*. It was written in 1087, just after William died.

> King William was stronger than any king before. He was so gentle to the good men and stern to those who disobeyed him. Also he was very violent, so that no-one dared to do anything against his will. The good peace he made in this country is not to be forgotten. An honest man could travel over his kingdom without injury with his pockets full of gold. William protected deer and boar and loved the stags so much as if he was their father. These things we have written about him, both good and bad, that good men may copy the good points and avoid the bad.

Is Source A a fair summary of William? You should consider the source's provenance and content, as well as reach your own conclusion.

....

....

....

....

.... [6]

Britain 1066–1509

The Norman Conquest

9 **a)** In what year did William Rufus succeed his father to become King of England?

.... [1]

b) Why was he called William Rufus?

.... [1]

c) How did William Rufus die?

....

....

.... [3]

10 Look carefully at the following photograph and answer the questions that follow. The photograph is of a modern replica of a medieval house in Mountfitchet, Essex.

a) Add the following labels to the photograph.

| toilet | water butt | no chimney | door | window |
[5]

b) How useful is a replica house like this to historians? Give **three** reasons.

....

....

.... [3]

c) What would it be like to live in a house like this?

....

....

.... [2]

11 How many peasants were living in England at the time of William the Conqueror?

.... [1]

12 How did they make a living?

....

....

.... [3]

13 Who owned all the land in the country?

.... [1]

14 a) How much land did the king keep for himself?

.... [1]

b) Who controlled the rest of the land? Give **two** groups of people.

....

.... [2]

15 What was this system of land ownership called?

.... [1]

16 How did the feudal system help William control England?

....

.... [2]

Total Marks .... / 51

Britain 1066–1509

Christendom and the Crusades

1 In which language were church services held? .... [1]

2 Why were church services held in this language? Give **three** reasons.

....

....

.... [3]

3 Why was the Church so rich and powerful?

....

....

....

.... [4]

4 Add these labels to the picture of a medieval monk.

| tonsure | cowl | girdle | habit | sandals |

[5]

5 Monks lived in monasteries, such as Whitby Abbey below.

What did monks do all day?

....

....

....

....

....

....

[5]

6 Why do you think people became monks or nuns?

....

....

....

[2]

7 What role did monks and nuns play in treating and helping the sick?

....

....

....

....

[4]

8 What role did monks play in spreading knowledge?

....

....

[2]

Total Marks .... / 26

Britain 1066–1509

This is a photograph of a stained-glass window in Canterbury Cathedral. It shows Thomas Becket, Archbishop of Canterbury. Answer the questions that follow.

1 Which role did Thomas Becket carry out for Henry II from 1155 onwards?

.... [1]

2 Which role did Thomas Becket carry out for Henry II from 1162 onwards?

.... [1]

3 What did Henry II and Thomas Becket quarrel about? Give **three** reasons.

....

....

....

.... [3]

4 What happened to Becket on 29 December 1170?

....

.... [2]

5 How did Henry say sorry for the death of Thomas Becket?

....

....

.... [3]

6 Study the following Victorian painting from 1875 of King John and Magna Carta and answer the question that follows.

How can you tell the artist thinks King John was a bad king?

_____

_____ [2]

7 Why was King John unpopular with the barons?

_____

_____

_____

_____ [3]

8 Why did the barons make John sign Magna Carta?

_____ [1]

9 a) What was the importance of Magna Carta for King John?

_____

_____ [2]

b) What was the importance of Magna Carta for the barons?

_____

_____ [2]

c) What was the importance of Magna Carta for ordinary people?

_____

_____ [2]

Total Marks _____ / 22

Britain 1066–1509

The Black Death

1 Fill the gaps in this paragraph with the correct words/numbers/years from the box below.

| 1349 | China | Weymouth | 30–45% | Italian | 1347 |

The Black Death originated in .... in .... From there it spread to the Black Sea. It was brought to Europe by .... merchants. Slowly it spread across Europe, arriving in England, at the port of ...., by early 1349. It spread across the whole country by the end of .... As much as .... of the population died from the Black Death.   [6]

2 Look carefully at this medieval painting, taken from a Bible, and answer the question that follows.

How can you tell the man and the woman have the plague?

....

.... [2]

3 Give **two** examples of things people did to try to avoid catching the Black Death.

....

.... [2]

4 Study the extract below, adapted from Henry Knighton's *Chronicon*, and answer the questions that follow. Henry Knighton was a priest who lived near Leicester and died in 1396. He wrote the following about the effects of the Black Death.

- Many buildings, large and small, had collapsed and completely fallen to the ground for lack of inhabitants …
- If anyone wanted to employ workers he had to pay them what they asked, or they would not work for him and he would lose his crops and fruit …
- There was everywhere such a great shortage of priests that many churches were abandoned …
- Many villages were completely deserted. All those who had lived there were dead …
- Everything became so dear that anything that in the past had been worth a penny was now worth four or five pence. And all foodstuffs became exceedingly dear …

a) According to Henry Knighton, what were **three** consequences of the Black Death in England?

_____

_____

_____ [3]

b) Which do you think Henry thought was the **most** important consequence of the Black Death? Why?

_____

_____ [2]

c) Which do you think Henry thought was the **least** important consequence of the Black Death? Why?

_____

_____ [2]

d) Which do you think was the **most** important consequence of the Black Death? Why?

_____

_____

_____ [3]

Total Marks _____ / 20

Britain 1066–1509

The Peasants' Revolt

Source A: Some modern historians describe the events of 1381.

> In 1381 thousands of angry people marched on London demanding to talk to the King. They were very angry about the taxes they were paying, especially the Poll Tax. They were also angry about disputes over land, rent rises and the impact of the Black Death. They killed tax collectors, destroyed paperwork, and executed the Treasurer and the Archbishop of Canterbury – both very important royal officials. This became known as the Peasants' Revolt.

1 What were the causes of the Peasants' Revolt?

....

....

....
[3]

2 Which of these people were more likely to take part in the Peasants' Revolt? Tick the correct answer(s).

Skilled workers ☐   Peasants ☐

The very poor who had no land ☐   Better-off farm workers ☐   [2]

3 How successful was the Peasants' Revolt?

....

....

....
[3]

4 Study Sources B and C and then answer the question that follows.

Source B: Criteria of someone or something that is significant, according to historian Ian Dawson.

> ### Significance
>
> According to historian Ian Dawson, someone or something is significant if it:
>
> - changed events at the time they lived
> - improved lots of people's lives – or made them worse
> - changed people's ideas
> - had a long-lasting impact on their country or the world
> - had been a really good or a very bad example to other people of how to live or behave.

Source C: An extract from a sermon by John Ball in London in 1381.

> When Adam delved and Eve span, who was then the gentleman? From the beginning all men by nature were created alike ...

John Ball was one of the leaders of the Peasants' Revolt. The peasants freed him from prison in Kent to go with them to London. From what you know of John Ball, how significant do you think he was in 1381? Use Ian Dawson's criteria to help you answer the question.

_____

_____

_____

_____

_____

[5]

5 The illustration below shows John Ball encouraging Wat Tyler (another leader of the Peasants' Revolt).

In your opinion, who was more impressive in London in 1381 – Wat Tyler or Richard II?

_____

_____

_____

_____

_____

[5]

Total Marks _____ / 18

Progress Test 1

1 From 1066 to 1265, if you didn't like what the king was doing, how could you make your voice heard?

.... [1]

2 Put the following monarchs in the order that they ruled England.

Henry II   Harold   William I   Richard II   John

....

....

....

....

.... [5]

3 Which **two** of these phrases best describe the life of a monk or nun? Tick the correct answers.

Make lots of money ☐

Life of chastity ☐

Get married and have children ☐

Wear very smart clothes ☐

Life of prayer ☐ [2]

4 Why was the Church so powerful in medieval times?

....

....

.... [3]

5 To what extent did the lives of rich and poor people change between Anglo-Saxon and Norman England? Explain your answer.

....

....

....

....

....

.... [5]

6 The following was expected of a medieval king:

- that he had a male heir to follow him as king
- that he kept everyone safe – people could travel the country and not get killed
- that he would keep the country safe from enemies
- that everyone – rich and poor – could get a fair trial in the law courts
- that he would listen to the views and ideas of the Church, and abide by the Church's rules.

Which of the medieval kings you have studied was, in your opinion, **most** successful in running the country?

....

....

....

....

....

[5]

7 The illustration below depicts a scene of medieval life.

Thomas Hobbes, writing in 1651, said that for most people, life was 'poor, nasty, brutish and short'. In what ways might this apply to ordinary people in medieval times?

....

....

....

....

....

[4]

Total Marks .... / 25

Reformation and Counter Reformation

The following images are stamps from 1997 showing Henry VIII and his six wives.

1 Why did Henry have six wives?

.... [1]

2 Why did Henry want to divorce his first wife, Catherine of Aragon, and why was this so difficult?

....

.... [2]

3 In which year did Henry make himself head of the Church in England?

.... [1]

4 Which **three** problems were important in causing Henry to split the Church in England from the Catholic Church?

....

....

.... [3]

5 Why did Henry VIII abolish the monasteries between 1536 and 1540?

....

....

.... [3]

6 If you went to church after 1547, what were the main changes you would have noticed?

....

....

.... [3]

7 Under Henry's son, Edward VI, the Church became more Protestant. When Mary I, who had been brought up a Catholic, became Queen, the Church returned to being Catholic. When Elizabeth I became Queen, the Church became Protestant again – although it was more tolerant of people having different views. It was all very confusing for people! Study Source A and answer the questions that follow.

Source A: Illustration in *Foxe's Book of Martyrs* showing the execution of the first Protestant martyr of Mary I's reign.

a) Source A is a drawing from a book published in 1563. What is happening in the illustration?

.... [1]

b) John Foxe was a Protestant. Does that make this source reliable?

....

.... [2]

8 Does Queen Mary, in your opinion, deserve the title 'Bloody Mary'?

....

....

....

.... [4]

Total Marks .... / 20

Britain 1509–1745

Causes of the English Civil War

1 When did Charles I become king?.. [1]

2 Charles believed in the Divine Right of Kings. What does this mean?

.... [1]

3 **a)** Why was religion a cause of the Civil War?

....

.... [2]

b) Why was money a cause of the Civil War?

....

.... [2]

c) Why was power a cause of the Civil War?

....

.... [2]

d) Which, in your opinion, was the most important cause of the Civil War? Why?

....

.... [2]

4 A Civil War army was made up of **three** main types of soldiers – pikemen, musketeers and cavalry. Anyone between the ages of **15** and **60** could be called to arms.

The two photographs show modern-day English Civil War re-enactors. Study the photos and then answer the questions that follow.

a) What was the job of the pikemen?

_____ [1]

b) What was the job of the musketeers?

_____ [1]

c) What was the job of the cavalry?

_____ [1]

5 The New Model Army was set up by Parliament in 1645 to help it win the war. How was it different from other armies?

_____

_____

_____

_____ [4]

6 During the war, many people's ideas changed. Some people talked about a 'world turned upside down'. One group was the Levellers. You can work out some of their ideas from their name. What political changes did they want?

_____

_____

_____ [3]

Total Marks _____ / 20

Britain 1509–1745

The Interregnum

The following image shows the execution of Charles I.

1 In which year was Charles I executed?

.... [1]

2 With the execution of the king, England became a republic. What does this mean?

.... [1]

3 Give **five** ways that Cromwell changed everyday life.

....

....

....

....

.... [5]

4 Did people feel better-off, or worse-off?

....

....

.... [3]

5 a) The following table compares Charles I and Cromwell. Put an 'x' in each appropriate
place to complete the table.

	Charles I	Cromwell
Was born to rule		
Believed Parliament should run the country		
Was a great general of the army		
Was indecisive – found it hard to make up his mind		
Wasn't very good at making speeches		
Was a Puritan		
Married a Catholic		
Died in his own bed		

[8]

The Interregnum

b) Who was more to blame for the English Civil War – Charles I or Oliver Cromwell?

....

....

....

[3]

6 The Interregnum [the name for a time 'between kings'] or Republic came to an end in 1660. Who was then invited to become King of England?

.... [1]

7 In which year did Charles I's son become King of England?

.... [1]

8 What was this new king's nickname?

.... [1]

9 How many illegitimate children did Charles II have?

.... [1]

10 How did Charles II take revenge on those who had executed his father?

....

....

....

[3]

11 How did Charles II change the role of the Church?

....

....

....

[3]

12 Give **one** reason Charles was a popular monarch.

.... [1]

13 Samuel Pepys lived in London and kept a diary from 1660 to 1669. It added up to 1,250,000 words! How useful is Samuel Pepys' *Diary* to historians?

....

....

....

....

....

[3]

14 Read Sources A and B and then answer the questions that follow.

Source A: Pepys' *Diary*, 13 October 1660.

> I went out to Charing Cross to see Major-General Harrison hanged, drawn and quartered he looking as cheerfully as any man could do in that condition. He was cut down and his head and his heart shown to the people, at which there were great shouts of joy.

Source B: Pepys' *Diary*, 16 October 1665.

> But Lord, how empty the streets are, so many poor sick people in the streets, full of sores, and so many sad stories overheard as I walk, everybody talking of this dead, and that man sick, and so many in this place, and so many in that. And they tell me that in Westminster there is never a physician [doctor] left, all being dead.

a) Which extract tells us most about London in the 1660s? Why?

....

....

....

[3]

b) Which extract tells us most about Samuel Pepys in the 1660s? Why?

....

....

....

[3]

15 Why did Samuel Pepys stop writing his *Diary* in 1669?

....

[1]

Total Marks .... / 42

Progress Test 2

1 When did the Civil War start?

.... [1]

2 What percentage of the English population died of the Black Death?

.... [1]

3 Name **three** important battles in the Civil War.

....

....

.... [3]

4 When did the Civil War end?

.... [1]

5 Add the labels in the box below to the photograph of pikemen taking part in a re-enactment.

pike	pot helmet	woollen breech
iron breastplate or leather corselet		wool stockings
	leather snapsack containing food and spare clothes	

[6]

6 What grievances did some people have with the Catholic Church?

....

....

....

.... [4]

7 What was the biggest problem Henry VIII faced?

.... [1]

8 Who do you think was the most successful monarch – William, John, Henry VIII or Charles I?

....

....

.... [3]

9 The illustration below shows the murder of Thomas Becket.

Where was Thomas Becket murdered?

.... [1]

10 What is the name given to the revolt against King Richard and the Poll Tax in 1381?

.... [1]

11 Put the monarchs on the timeline in the order that they ruled England.

Mary	Harold	Charles II	William I	John	Henry VIII
	Richard II	Edward VI	Henry II	Elizabeth I	Charles I

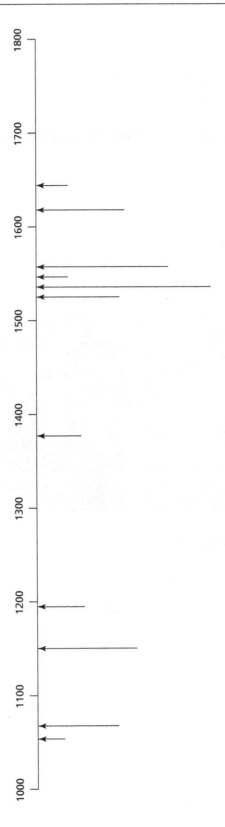

[11]

12 How similar were the problems faced by King John with the barons to those faced by Charles I and Parliament?

....

....

....

....

.... [5]

13 The photograph below shows the medieval church in Arreton on the Isle of Wight.

In medieval times, what language were church services held in?

.... [1]

14 Who was Henry Knighton and why do we remember him?

....

.... [2]

15 What was a 'flagellant'?

....

.... [1]

16 What does the word 'Interregnum' mean?

.... [1]

Total Marks .... / 43

Britain 1745–1901

British Transatlantic Slave Trade

1 When were the first African slaves shipped to the Americas? .... [1]

2 Why was there such a demand for African slaves in the Americas?

....

....

.... [3]

3 What did Europeans think about Africans?

....

.... [2]

4 Look carefully at the engraving below, which was made in 1859, and then answer the questions that follow.

a) What does the engraving show?

....

.... [2]

b) The engraving was made in 1859. How useful is it to us as evidence of the slave trade?

....

.... [2]

5 The photograph below shows a plaque on a house in Wisbech, Cambridgeshire dedicated to Thomas Clarkson.

What part did Thomas Clarkson play in the abolition of the slave trade?

....

.... [2]

6 When was the slave trade via British ships abolished? .... [1]

7 Why was there so much opposition to abolition of the slave trade?

....

.... [2]

8 What part did Olaudah Equiano (below) play in the abolition of the slave trade?

....

....

.... [2]

9 Who do you think was more important in the abolition of slavery – Clarkson or Equiano? Why?

....

....

.... [3]

> **Total Marks** .... / 20

Britain 1745–1901

Britain as the First Industrial Nation

1 What was Richard Arkwright's first job? .... [1]

2 When did he open his first factory? .... [1]

3 Why did he build his first factory in Cromford?

....

.... [2]

4 The photograph below shows some cottages built by Richard Arkwright for workers at his factory in Cromford. Look carefully at the photograph and then answer the questions that follow.

a) Add the following labels to the photograph:

door	chimney	windows	roof

[2]

b) How can you tell this is a modern photograph?

.... [1]

c) Why do you think the third floor has more windows than any other floor?

....

.... [2]

5 How did Arkwright get his cloth to Manchester?

.... [1]

6 Why were the new industrial cities so unpleasant to live in?

....

....

....

....

.... [5]

7 Most people at the time thought disease was spread by the miasma theory.
What does this mean?

....

.... [2]

8 How **similar** were the 1848 Public Health Act and the 1875 Public Health Act?

....

....

.... [3]

9 Read Source A and answer the questions that follow.

Source A: Extract from an interview with John Reed, factory worker, in 1842.

I went to work at the cotton factory of Messrs Arkwright at the age of nine. I was then a fine strong, healthy lad, and straight in every limb. I earned 2s [10p] per week at first, for 72 hours' work. I continued to work in this factory for 10 years, getting gradually higher wages, till I had 6s. 3d. per week; which is the highest wages I ever had. I gradually became a cripple, till at the age of 19 I was unable to stand at the machine, and I was forced to give it up. I have been made a miserable cripple, as you see, and cast off by those who had benefited from my labour, without a single penny.

a) What did John Reed do?

.... [1]

Britain as the First Industrial Nation

b) How much did he earn when he was nine years old?

.... [1]

c) How much did he earn when he was 19 years old?

.... [1]

10 What effect did working have on John Reed?

....

.... [2]

11 If conditions were so bad, why did people work in the factories?

....

.... [2]

12 Gradually the government passed laws making working conditions better. Match the laws made by the government with the improvement they introduced to factory work.

Factory Act		Improvement made
1819 Cotton Mills and Factories Act		Limited the hours children could work in factories and introduced the first factory inspectors
1833 Factory Act		Limited the hours women and children could work to 10 hours a day
1847 Factory Act		Children under nine were not allowed to work in factories, and children aged 9–16 could only work for 12 hours per day

[3]

13 In Victorian times countries wanted to have an empire. Why?

....

.... [2]

14 Which country had the biggest empire in Victorian times? Tick the correct answer.

Britain ☐   Italy ☐

France ☐   Spain ☐

Germany ☐   USA ☐   [1]

15 Look at the map below of the British Empire in Victorian times and complete the tasks that follow.

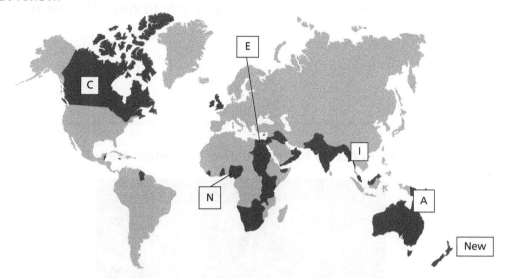

Some of Britain's colonies have been identified on the map. Complete the names of the colonies below and add the main product/raw material that each country sent to Britain.

cotton	lamb	wheat	tea	wool	palm oil

Country	Product/raw material
C..	....
N..	....
E..	....
I..	....
A..	....
New......................................	....

[6]

16 What percentage of the world's population lived in the British Empire in 1870?

.... [1]

Total Marks .... / 40

Britain 1745–1901

Democratic Reform

1 Which **three** conditions did you have to meet to be able to vote after the 1832 Great Reform Act?

....

....

.... [3]

2 How did the 1832 Reform Act try to make the voting system fairer?

....

....

.... [3]

3 Who were the Chartists?

....

.... [2]

4 How did the government respond to the demands of the Chartists?

....

.... [2]

5 How did the 1867 Reform Act change who could vote?

....

.... [2]

6 What was important about the 1872 Act?

....

.... [2]

7 What was important about the 1884 Reform Act?

....

.... [2]

8 How many of the Chartist's six demands had been met by 1884?

A vote for every male aged 21 and over
Secret ballots
Payment for MPs
No property qualifications
Annual parliaments
Equal constituencies

.... [1]

9 How democratic, in your opinion, was Britain in 1884?

....

....

.... [3]

Total Marks .... / 20

Progress Test 3

1 Who had the most power to rule the country? Tick your answer and give **two** reasons for your choice.

King William in 1067 ☐

King John in 1215 ☐

King Richard II in 1381 ☐

King Charles I in 1642 ☐

Queen Victoria in 1884 ☐

....

....

.... [3]

2 Historians argue that the 1875 Public Health Act was a turning point in government attitudes to social reform. How?

....

.... [2]

3 When was slavery abolished throughout the British Empire?

.... [1]

4 a) How many people worked making cotton in 1838?

.... [1]

b) How many people worked making cotton in 1885?

.... [1]

5 What replaced canals as the best way to transport goods and people?

.... [1]

6 Who was not allowed to vote despite the reforms up to 1884?

....

.... [2]

7 How many slaves are thought to have been taken from Africa to the Americas by Europeans?

.... [1]

8 Historians often call the Victorian period the Great Changes.

a) Which do you think was the greatest change during this period? Circle your answer.

Abolition of slavery	New factories	Canals and railways
More people live in cities not the countryside		
More people work in industry not agriculture		More people can vote

[1]

b) List these changes in their order of importance – most important at the top; least important at the bottom.

_____

_____

_____

_____

_____

_____

[3]

c) Explain why you have chosen **one** of these as most important.

_____

_____

_____

[3]

9 In which year were local councils **forced** to act to improve public health in the new industrial cities?

_____

[1]

10 a) How many men could vote in 1884?

_____

[1]

b) How many women could vote in 1884?

_____

[1]

11 Put the following monarchs in the order they ruled England/Britain on the timeline.

Victoria	William I	Henry VIII
Elizabeth I	Harold	Henry II	Richard II
Mary	John	Charles I	Charles II	Edward VI

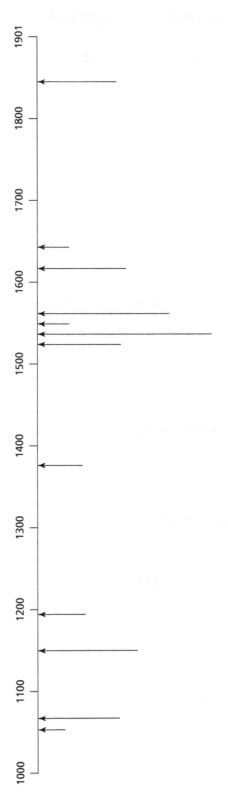

[12]

12 When was slavery abolished in the USA?

.... [3]

13 What religion was John Foxe?

.... [1]

14 Which, in your opinion, was the most important Reform Act in the 19th century – 1832, 1867, 1872 or 1884? Why?

....

....

....

.... [4]

15 a) Who was the last Anglo-Saxon king of England?

.... [1]

b) When did he die?

.... [1]

16 How similar were the Black Death of 1347 and the cholera epidemic of 1848?

....

....

....

....

.... [5]

17 What replaced water power in the new factories?

.... [1]

Total Marks .... / 50

Britain 1901–Present

Women's Suffrage

The following image is of a British stamp showing a statue of Emmeline Pankhurst, issued to commemorate the 50th anniversary of women's suffrage. Study the image and answer the questions that follow.

1 Why was it assumed that women did not need the vote?

_____

_____ [2]

2 Besides voting, name **two** other things women could not do in Victorian times.

_____

_____ [2]

3 a) What was seen as a woman's role?

_____ [1]

b) Which women found this difficult to do?

_____

_____ [2]

4 Which of these rights were given to women in the 1870s and 1880s? Circle the answers.

Right to vote	**Right to keep their own income when they married**
	Right to get a divorce more easily
Right to stand as an MP	**Equal pay for equal work**
	Right to keep their own property when they married

[2]

5 Which organisation was set up in 1897 to try to get the vote for women?

_____ [1]

6 Who was the leader of the the National Union of Women's Suffrage Societies (NUWSS)?

.... [1]

7 The Women's Social and Political Union (WSPU) was set up in 1903. Who was its leader?

.... [1]

8 Which suffrage group used which tactics? Put an 'x' in each appropriate place to complete the table.

Tactics	NUWSS	WSPU
Had a slogan, 'Deeds not Words'		
Wanted only richer women who owned property to have the vote		
Used peaceful, persuasive tactics in an attempt to persuade MPs to give them the vote		
Used violent methods, such as putting bombs in post boxes and breaking windows, to publicise the issue of women's suffrage		
Disrupted political meetings to get publicity		

[5]

9 Read Source A, which was written by a modern historian, and then answer the questions that follow.

Source A:

> The women's suffrage movement was a watershed in British women's history. It brought women together in a mass movement unparalleled in British history. It was successful in gaining equal voting rights for women, the right of women to be elected to Parliament, and contributed to the admission of women to political parties. But it did not bring radical change. They could vote, but what else had changed?

a) This is a secondary source – does that make it reliable?

.... [1]

b) Do you agree with the conclusion that nothing had really changed?

....

.... [2]

Total Marks .... / 20

Britain 1901–Present

1. On 28 June 1914 Archduke Franz Ferdinand was assassinated in Sarajevo. This led to the start of the First World War. Using the labels provided in the box, complete the table of the **main** participants in the war in 1914.

| Austria-Hungary | France | Russia | Germany | Great Britain |

Allied powers	Central powers

[5]

2. The map below shows the countries at war in December 1914. Look carefully at the map and answer the question that follows.

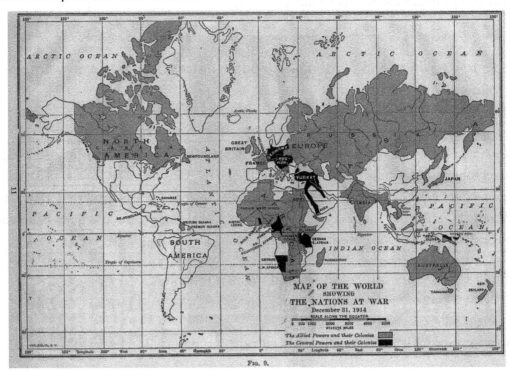

FIG. 9.

Does the map help to explain why the war was called a **world** war?

....

....

....

[3]

3 How did the war impact on people at home in Britain, on the 'Home Front'?

....

.... [2]

4 The photograph below is of a modern memorial to the Birmingham Pals Battalion. Look carefully at the picture and answer the questions that follow.

a) What were 'Pals' Battalions?

....

....

.... [1]

b) Give **one** reason why this was a good idea.

.... [1]

c) Give **one** reason why this might be a bad idea.

.... [1]

5 This illustration was published in a newspaper during the First World War. It shows the Somme offensive, the taking of Longueval, on 28 July 1916. Look carefully at the picture and answer the questions that follow.

a) How can you tell the soldiers are Scottish?

.... [1]

The First World War

b) How realistic do you think it is?

....

....

.... [3]

c) How useful is this source in telling us about conditions in the trenches in 1916?

....

....

.... [3]

6 Look carefully at the photograph below and answer the questions that follow.

a) The photograph shows a new weapon introduced in 1916. What was it called?

.... [1]

b) Give **two** ways this new weapon could make life safer for soldiers.

....

.... [2]

c) Give **two** ways this new weapon could make life more dangerous for soldiers.

....

.... [2]

7 Three other new weapons were developed during the war. Complete the table giving **one** way each of these weapons made the war more dangerous for soldiers.

New weapon	Impact
Gas	
Machine guns	
Aircraft	

[3]

8 Which of these new weapons, in your opinion, had the greatest impact on trench warfare?

....

.... [2]

9 The First World War ended on 11 November 1918 with an agreed ceasefire. The treaty which ended the war with Germany, signed in June 1919, was called what?

.... [1]

10 Name **four** major terms of the treaty that Germany hated.

....

....

....

.... [4]

11 Study the photograph of a war memorial and answer the questions that follow.

a) How many men from the village died in the war?

.... [1]

b) Where did they die?

....

.... [2]

c) How useful is this war memorial in telling us about the cost of the First World War?

....

.... [2]

TO THE GLORIOUS DEAD
AND IN HONOURED MEMORY OF
THE MEN OF LITTLE HALE,
WHO GAVE THEIR LIVES IN
THE GREAT WAR 1914 – 1919,
FRED CARRILL,
AT SUVLA BAY, AUG, 9TH 1915,
AGED 18 YEARS.
JOHN WILLIAM WARD,
AT YPRES, OCT, 4TH 1917,
AGED 27 YEARS.

Total Marks .... / 37

Britain 1901–Present

1 Use the list of words in the box to complete the paragraph below about the start of the Second World War.

Austria	the Sudetenland	appeasement
army	great power	Adolf Hitler	Treaty of Versailles

In 1933, ... came to power in Germany. He was determined to make Germany a .... again by tearing up the .... and building up Germany's .... In 1938 he took over .... and .... [which was part of Czechoslovakia]. No country was prepared to stand up to him. This policy was called .... [7]

2 The Second World War started when Germany invaded Poland in which year?
.... [1]

3 Why did appeasement fail?

....

.... [2]

4 Put numbers 1–5 in the boxes beside these events to place them in the correct chronological order, with 1 being the oldest.

V1 and V2 rockets attack Britain ☐

Evacuation of children from the cities and towns ☐

Blitz ☐

VE Day ☐

Battle of Britain ☐ [5]

5 Look carefully at this photograph, taken in England in 1943, and answer the questions that follow.

a) What is happening in the photograph?

....

.... [1]

b) Why are there only old people in the photograph?

....

.... [1]

c) How useful is a photograph like this for telling us about life in Britain during the Second World War?

....

....

....

....

.... [3]

6 Until 1942 it seemed that Germany and her allies were winning the war. Gradually, from 1942 onwards, things began to change. There were several key 'turning points' in the war when Britain and her allies began to gain the advantage.

Use the labels in the boxes to complete the table on page 50.

Month/year

August 1942–February 1943	**1943–44**
June 1942 **June 1944** **October–November 1942**	

Significant event

Russian troops stop German advance into the Soviet Union

American and British navies stop German submarines sinking supply ships

US troops stop the Japanese advance in the Pacific

British, American and Canadian troops land in Europe and begin to recapture France

Britain and her allies stop the German advance in North Africa

Britain 1901–Present

Battle	Month/year	Significant event
Midway		
El Alamein		
Stalingrad		
Atlantic		
D-Day		

[10]

7 Look at the painting below by a German artist, which was painted in 1941, and answer the questions that follow.

a) What is happening in the picture?

_____ [1]

b) Why were German submarines, or U-boats, such a threat to Britain during the Second World War?

_____ [1]

8 What did Adolf Hitler do on 30 April 1945?

.... [1]

9 8 May 1945 is known as VE day. What does 'VE' stand for?

.... [1]

10 Which new weapon was dropped on Hiroshima on 6 August 1945?

.... [1]

11 Study Sources A and B and answer the question that follows.

Source A: Photograph showing the centre of Hiroshima on 6 August 1945.

Source B: An extract written by a modern historian.

The decision to drop the atomic bomb was made by US President Truman who argued that it would shorten the war, remove any need to invade Japan itself and so save the lives of thousands of American servicemen as well as Japanese civilians.

How useful are the sources to a historian studying the atomic bomb that was dropped on Hiroshima in August 1945?

....

.... [2]

12 When did the Second World War end?

.... [1]

Total Marks .... / 37

Creation of the Welfare State

1 According to Charles Booth, what percentage of people living in London in 1902 lived below the poverty line? .... [1]

2 According to Seebohm Rowntree, what percentage of people living in York in 1899 lived below the poverty line? .... [1]

3 Why did the Liberal Government of 1906–11 decide to do something about poverty and ill health?

....

....

.... [3]

4 At which **three** stages of life did Booth say people were most vulnerable and in need of most help?

....

....

.... [3]

5 Name **two** things the Liberal Government introduced to help tackle these problems.

....

.... [2]

6 During the Second World War, Beveridge published a report showing the problems Britain would face after the war. What year was it published? .... [1]

7 Beveridge talked about the 'Five Giants of Evil'. These were want, disease, squalor, ignorance and idleness. Complete the table saying why each of these was a problem.

'Giant'	Problems this caused
Want	
Disease	
Squalor	
Ignorance	
Idleness	

[5]

8 How similar were the problems identified by Beveridge to those identified by Booth and Rowntree?

....

.... [2]

9 Which, in your opinion, improved life most for ordinary people – the Liberal Reforms of 1906–11 or the Labour Reforms of 1945–50 based on Beveridge's Report?

....

.... [2]

Total Marks .... / 20

Britain 1901–Present

Britain's Place in the World 1945–Present

1 **Source A:** Harold Macmillan, British Prime Minister, speaking in 1957.

> ... let us be frank about it – most of our people have never had it so good. Go around the country, go to the industrial towns, go to the farms and you will see a state of prosperity such as we have never had in my lifetime – nor indeed in the history of this country.

a) Do you agree that in 1957 Britons had 'never had it so good'?

....

.... [2]

b) How useful is this speech in telling us about working life in the 1950s?

....

....

.... [3]

2 What was the 'Winter of Discontent'?

....

.... [2]

3 Name **two** ways in which employment has changed since 1957.

....

....

.... [3]

4 Look at the photograph below and answer the questions that follow.

a) Which of these would you be **most likely** to find in the average home in the 1940s?

.... [1]

b) Which of these would you be **most likely** to find in the average home in the 1970s?

....

.... [4]

c) Which of these would you be **most likely** to find in the average home today?

.... [1]

5 **a)** How many women were employed outside the home by the 1990s?

.... [1]

b) How had this changed since the 1940s?

.... [1]

6 Who was Britain's first female Prime Minister?

.... [1]

7 Which of the following, in your opinion, has had the greatest impact on social life since the end of the Second World War? Tick your answer and explain why you made this choice.

The contraceptive pill ☐

Central heating ☐

The Internet ☐

Reducing the voting age to 18 ☐

Indoor plumbing ☐

Legalising abortion ☐

Legalising homosexuality ☐

....

.... [2]

Total Marks .... / 21

1. When would you have preferred to live – medieval England, Tudor England, Victorian England, or before the Second World War? Explain why you made this choice.

....

....

.... [2]

2. Who were the most militant when trying to get women the vote, Suffragists or Suffragettes?

.... [1]

3. Which king of England ruled for the longest part of the year 1066?

.... [1]

4. Which German attack on Britain lasted from September 1940 until
May 1941? .... [1]

5. What was the name of the first railway?

.... [1]

6. How similar were armies in the English Civil War and the First World War?

....

....

....

....

.... [5]

7. In what ways did the Labour Government of 1945–51 make life better for most people?

....

....

....

....

.... [5]

8. a) What was the population of the UK in 1948? .... [1]

   b) What was the population of the UK in 1997? .... [1]

   c) What is the population of the UK in 2020? .... [1]

   d) How do you explain these changes?

....

.... [2]

9 Who was Prime Minister in 1957 and said 'most of our people have never had it so good'?

.... [1]

10 Put the following monarchs in the order that they ruled England/Britain by numbering them 1–15.

Henry VIII	☐	Mary	☐
Elizabeth I	☐	Charles II	☐
Harold	☐	Edward VI	☐
Edward VII	☐	George VI	☐
Charles I	☐	John	☐
William I	☐	Richard II	☐
Elizabeth II	☐	Victoria	☐ [15]
Henry II	☐		

11 What happened on 11 November 1918? .... [1]

12 How many wives did Henry VIII have? .... [1]

13 When was England a republic? .... [1]

14 Who led the Peasants' Revolt against King Richard II? .... [1]

15 Which countries fought each other on the Eastern Front in the First World War?

....

.... [2]

16 Put numbers 1–3 in the boxes beside these protest groups to place them in the correct chronological order, with 1 being the oldest.

Chartists ☐

Martin Luther and the Protestants ☐

Suffragettes ☐ [3]

17 a) When was D-Day? .... [1]

b) What was its significance?

....

....

.... [3]

Total Marks .... / 50

British Social History

Migration To and From the British Isles

1 The 1948 Nationality Act allowed who to come and live in Britain?

.... [1]

2 Why did firms like London Transport and the NHS encourage migrants to come and live and work in Britain?

....

.... [2]

3 Look closely at the advertisement from a newspaper in Kingston, Jamaica, from 15 April 1948 and answer the questions that follow.

> ## Passenger Opportunity
> ## To United Kingdom
> Troopship "EMPIRE WINDRUSH" sailing
> about 23rd MAY.
> Fares:— Cabin Class **£43**
> Troopdeck **£28**
> Royal Mail Lines, Limited—8 Port Royal St.

a) How much was the cheapest fare from the West Indies to London?

.... [1]

b) What kind of ship was the *Empire Windrush*? How can you tell?

....

.... [2]

c) How comfortable do you think 'troopdeck' accommodation was?

.... [1]

4 Name **three** difficulties these early migrants faced when they arrived in Britain.

....

....

.... [3]

5 Experts talk about 'push' factors and 'pull' factors as causes of migration. Put an 'x' in each appropriate place to complete the table.

Reason to migrate	Push factor	Pull factor
War		
Better education		
Poverty		
Better standard of living		
Lack of opportunity in native country		

[5]

6 Since the 1960s there have been more immigrants to Britain than emigrants from Britain. Name **two** parts of the world many of these immigrants have come from.

[2]

7 When Britain joined the European Union, and agreed to free migration within Europe, where did most migrants to the UK come from?

[2]

8 Give **two** major ways immigration has, in your opinion, made Britain a better place.

[2]

9 If you were leaving Britain to live in a new country, and could only take one suitcase, what would you take with you?

[3]

10 Which politician made the 'Rivers of Blood' speech in April 1968, warning about the dangers of unrestricted immigration?

[1]

British Social History

11 Look closely at the figures for emigration and immigration in the table below.

Decade	Emigration	Immigration
1920–29	3,960,000	2,590,000
1930–39	2,273,000	2,361,000
1940–49	590,000	240,000
1950–59	1,327,000	676,000
1960–69	1,916,000	1,243,000
1970–79	2,554,000	1,900,000

Source: Michael Lynch, *An introduction to Modern British History 1900–1999.*

a) From your knowledge of Britain in the 20th century, why was emigration so high in the 1920s and 1930s, and so low in the 1940s?

....

....

.... [3]

b) Which countries did most of the emigrants go to?

....

.... [4]

12 How much did an Assisted Package cost in the 1960s?

.... [2]

13 Why did people think immigration was a problem?

....

....

....

.... [2]

14 Why did some people think emigration was a problem?

....

.... [2]

15 Parliament introduced several Acts of Parliament restricting immigration. Draw lines to match each Act with its actions.

1962 Commonwealth Immigration Act	You must already have a job to be admitted to Britain as an immigrant AND you must have parent or grandparent living in the UK
1965 Race Relations Act	Banned discrimination in employment and in housing
1968 Commonwealth Immigrants Act	Made it illegal to incite racial hatred
1968 Race Relations Act	Immigrants needed a one-year work permit to be able to come and live and work in the UK
1971 Immigration Act	You must already have a job to be admitted to Britain as an immigrant

[5]

16 Is it fair to say that by 1971 immigrants were treated more fairly in Britain?

....

.... [2]

Total Marks .... / 45

World History

USA in the 20th Century

1 Which industries were growing rapidly in the USA in the 1920s?

_____

_____

_____ **[3]**

2 Which industries were doing badly in the USA in the 1920s?

_____ **[2]**

3 How could people afford to buy these new goods?

_____ **[1]**

4 Which organisation had 4 million members in 1925 and tried to make life very difficult for African-Americans?

_____ **[1]**

5 The photograph below is of someone in their motor car in the 1920s. Study the photograph carefully and then answer the questions that follow.

a) Is this photograph primary or secondary evidence?

_____ **[1]**

b) How useful is it in helping us find out about the USA in the 1920s?

_____

_____ **[2]**

6 Read Source A carefully and then answer the questions that follow.

Source A: A modern historian's view.

> The strength of America's economy in the 1920s came to a sudden end in October 1929. Suddenly the 'glamour' of the Jazz Age and gangsters disappeared and America was faced with a major crisis that was to impact countries as far away as Germany – a nation that had built its economy on American loans.

a) Which event brought the strength of America's economy to a sudden end?

.... [1]

b) Why were countries like Germany affected by this event?

.... [1]

c) Did everybody in America benefit from the 'glamour' of the Jazz Age?

....

.... [2]

7 How many people were unemployed in the USA in 1932? .... [1]

8 How many banks closed down in the USA after the Wall Street Crash?

.... [1]

9 Study the photograph below of migrant workers picking carrots in California in 1938 and then answer the questions that follow.

World History

USA in the 20th Century

a) Is the photograph primary or secondary evidence? .... [1]

b) The photograph was taken in 1938. Does it prove that America's economy was back on track by then?

....

....

.... [3]

10 North Vietnam was a Communist country. Why did this worry the USA?

.... [1]

11 When did America send troops to fight in Vietnam? .... [1]

12 Study the photograph below and then answer the question that follows.

What is happening in the photograph?

....

....

....

.... [2]

13 Why was the Vietnam War so unpopular in the USA?

....

....

....

....

.... [5]

14 When did the Vietnam War end? .... [1]

15 In most states in the South of the USA, African-Americans and white people had separate schools, restaurants and public toilets. What was this policy known as?

.... [1]

16 In 1955, Rosa Parks did what in protest at this policy and what did it lead to?

....

.... [2]

17 What is this type of protest known as? .... [1]

18 Study the photograph below of Dr Martin Luther King giving a speech in Washington D.C. in 1963 and then answer the question that follows.

How many people marched to Washington D.C. to listen to Dr Martin Luther King speak?

_____ [1]

19 Read **Source B**, which is an extract from Dr Martin Luther King's 'I have a dream' speech in Washington in August 1963, and then answer the question that follows.

Source B:

> I have a dream that my four little children will one day live in a nation where they will not be judged by the color of their skin, but by the content of their character. I have a dream today!

What dream did Dr Martin Luther King have?

_____ [1]

20 Complete the following table by adding what was changed by each of the Acts listed.

Act	What the Act did
1964 Civil Rights Act	
1965 Voting Rights Act	

[2]

21 How important was Dr Martin Luther King in the struggle for equality and freedom for African-Americans?

_____

_____ [2]

Progress Test 5

1 What was 'great' about the Great Reform Act of 1832?

....

....

.... [3]

2 Which country did the immigrants on the *Empire Windrush* travel from in 1948?

.... [1]

3 Give **one** example of a 'push' factor causing people to move from one country to another.

.... [1]

4 How similar were the UK and the USA in the 1930s?

....

....

.... [3]

5 Give **one** example of a 'pull' factor causing people to move from one country to another.

.... [1]

6 In the 1960s and 1970s, which part of the world did most migrants to the UK come from?

.... [1]

7 Which groups were evacuated from London and other cities at the start of the Second World War?

.... [1]

8 Throughout the 20th century, which has been greater, emigration from or immigration to Britain?

.... [1]

9 Why did Prohibition make the USA less law-abiding?

....

.... [2]

10 Who was President of the USA from 1932–45? .... [1]

11 What did he do to try to get America back to work?

....

....

.... [3]

12 In the 21st century, which part of the world do most migrants to Britain come from?

.... [1]

13 How do most historians think the Black Death was spread?

.... [1]

14 Why did the USA fight a war in Vietnam?

.... [1]

15 Name the **two** main employers that helped immigrants come to Britain in the 1950s.

.... [2]

16 In America, what was 'the draft'?

.... [1]

17 To what extent were African-Americans equal to white Americans by 1965?

....

.... [2]

18 Put these wars in the correct sequence by adding numbers 1–5 in the boxes, with 1 being the oldest.

The Great War	☐	Vietnam War	☐
English Civil War	☐	American War of Independence	☐
Crimean War	☐		[5]

19 Who took the blame for the death of Thomas Becket? .... [1]

20 Which women could vote in Britain by 1928?

.... [1]

21 a) Which **one** of these people was female in the medieval Church? Circle the correct answer.

monk	nun	priest	bishop	archbishop	abbot

[1]

b) Which of these people might be female in the Church today? Circle the correct answers.

monk	nun	priest	bishop	archbishop	abbot

[4]

22 Where was Richard Arkwright's first textile factory built in 1771?

.... [1]

23 a) What was the name of the law that was passed in the USA that made it illegal for people to buy alcohol?

.... [1]

b) During this time in America, where did people go in order to get an alcoholic drink?

.... [1]

Total Marks .... / 41

Mixed Test-Style Questions

Choose just **one** question to answer. Each question is worth 5 marks.

1 Study the source below, which is a 15th-century German image showing the impact of the Black Death.

How is this source useful in helping you to explain why people were afraid of the Black Death? How is it less useful? Remember to look at what the source shows/tells you and what it does not.

Give reasons for your answer.

2 Study the source below, which is a modern historian's view of the Peasants' Revolt.

> Richard II bravely rode up to the rebels. They wanted revenge for their leader's death and were preparing for battle. Calmly he asked them what was wrong and told them he was their king and they should follow him. And the Peasants' Revolt ended and the rebels went home.

How useful is this source in explaining the end of the Peasants' Revolt?

Explain your answer.

Mixed Test-Style Questions

Choose just **one** question to answer. Each question is worth 5 marks.

1 Study the source below about Queen Elizabeth I. It was written by Pope Sixtus V, who led the Catholic Church from 1585 till his death in 1590.

> She is a great Queen and were she only a Catholic she would be our dearly beloved. Just look at how well she governs! She is only a woman and yet she makes herself feared by Spain, by France, by all.

How useful is this source in helping us to understand the problems Elizabeth faced as Queen of England?

2 Study the source below. It is a picture of a modern statue of Oliver Cromwell erected in 1899 outside the Houses of Parliament in London.

What can we tell about Cromwell from the statue?

Mixed Test-Style Questions

Choose just **one** question to answer. Each question is worth 5 marks.

1 Read Heinrich Heine's statement below. Heine died in 1856.

> Railways are nothing but a device for making the world smaller.

To what extent do you agree with Heine's statement?

2 Look at this modern photograph of a Victorian workhouse in Southwell, Nottinghamshire.

How useful is this photograph in helping us to understand what it was like to live in a Victorian workhouse?

_____

_____

_____

_____

_____

_____

Mixed Test-Style Questions

Choose just **one** question to answer. Each question is worth 5 marks.

1 Study the following photograph, which shows the inside of a French dugout in Verdun in 1916.

Is this photograph typical of life in the trenches during the First World War?

2 In his memoirs after the Second World War, Winston Churchill wrote the following:

> … the only thing that ever really frightened me during the war was the U-boat peril …

Do you agree with Churchill that the U-boat peril was the most frightening aspect of the war? Support your answer with evidence.

....

....

....

....

....

....

....

Mixed Test-Style Questions

Choose just **one** question to answer. Each question is worth 5 marks.

1 Look carefully at the *Punch* cartoon from 1954 below.

How useful is this source in helping us to understand migration after World War Two?

2 Read the source below carefully. It is a modern historian's view of Britain in the 1960s.

> The emergence of teen culture in the 1960s changed Britain. Teenagers had previously listened to their parents' music of the 1940s. The Beatles and the Rolling Stones gave teenagers a sense of their own identity and helped to make attitudes more liberal, particularly towards women. The pill was introduced and abortion was legalised. Pop music also had an influence on changing styles of dance and fashion. A musical and social revolution was born.

Use this source and your own knowledge to explain how life changed in Britain in the 1960s.

....

....

....

....

Mixed Test-Style Questions

Choose just **one** question to answer. Each question is worth 10 marks.

1 How and why did William build castles all over the country after he became King of England? Support your answer with evidence.

2 Read what Henrietta Marshall, writing in 1908 in *Our Island Story*, had to say about King John.

> No king of England has ever been so bad as John. He was a bad son, a bad brother, a bad king and a bad man.

Do you agree with her assessment of King John? Support your answer with evidence.

3 How secure was life for a medieval peasant? Support your answer with evidence.

[Continue your answer on a separate piece of paper.]

Choose just **one** question to answer. Each question is worth 10 marks.

1 Explain why some people describe the period of the Civil War as 'the world turned upside down'. Use evidence to support your answer.

2 Explain why the Church caused such bitter arguments in Britain in Tudor times. Use evidence to support your answer.

3 Explain why most people were pleased to see Charles II restored as King of England in 1660. Use evidence to support your answer.

[Continue your answer on a separate piece of paper.]

Mixed Test-Style Questions

Choose just **one** question to answer. Each question is worth 10 marks.

1. What was 'great' about the Great Exhibition of 1851? Use evidence to support your answer.

2. Was Titus Salt a typical factory owner? Use evidence to support your answer.

3. Explain how and why entertainment changed during Queen Victoria's reign. Use evidence to support your answer.

[Continue your answer on a separate piece of paper.]

Choose just **one** question to answer. Each question is worth 10 marks.

1. How should we remember Margaret Thatcher?

2. Should the atomic bomb have been dropped on Hiroshima in August 1945?

3. Explain the impact the development of the Welfare State in Britain after 1945 had on the lives of ordinary people.

[Continue your answer on a separate piece of paper.]

Mixed Test-Style Questions

Choose just **one** question to answer. Each question is worth 10 marks.

1. Explain why the USA went from 'boom' to 'bust' in the 1920s and 1930s. Support your answer with evidence.

2. How important was Dr Martin Luther King in the fight for Civil Rights in America in the 1950s and 1960s? Support your answer with evidence.

3. Why was the Vietnam War so unpopular in America? Support your answer with evidence.

[Continue your answer on a separate piece of paper.]

Answers

Britain 1066–1509

Pages 4–7 The Norman Conquest

1. Edward the Confessor [1]; Harold Godwinson [1]; William [1]
2. I think.. had the best claim
   because.. . **[Each statement gains 1 mark, maximum of 2 marks]**
   Example answers:
   Harold: he was the most powerful man in the country; he was Edward's brother-in-law; chosen as king by the Witan when Edward died; commander of the Saxon army and had the support of the nobility; had been running the country when Edward was old and infirm; he was a Saxon; Harold said that Edward had promised him the throne whilst on his deathbed. **[Any three points for 3 marks + previous two statements, for a maximum of 5 marks]**
   William: William claimed that Harold has promised to support his claim in 1064; the Pope supported his claim; he was Edward's cousin; William claimed that Edward had promised him the throne in 1051. **[Any three points for 3 marks + previous two statements, for a maximum of 5 marks]**
3. Hastings [1]
4. William [1]
5. The Domesday Book [1]
6. Any three from: to find out who owned what; to discover how landholding had changed since 1066; to know how much to tax people; to pay for his army; he was running out of money. [3]
7. Very: it is (nearly) from William's lifetime [1]; people who fought in the battle told the story to those who made the tapestry. [1] Not very: it was made by the Normans so tells the story from one side only [1]; it was made to celebrate the victory, not to tell us what happened. [1] In conclusion........................ .[1] **[You must reach a conclusion to gain the final mark.]**
8. Answers should include both provenance and content: an Anglo-Saxon monk wrote it [1]; so it might be one-sided [1]; it says **mostly** only nice things about him [1]; but it does say he was violent [1]; reach a conclusion related to both provenance and content for the final 2 marks. [2]
9. a) 1087 [1]
   b) Because of his red hair and his fiery temper [1]
   c) He was shot by an arrow [1]; in a hunting accident [1]; or perhaps not – he was so unpopular his death may not have been an accident. [1]
10. a)
    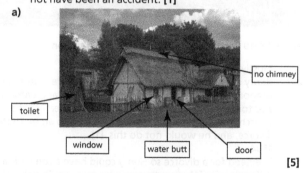
    [5]
    b) Any three from: Very: if it is based on careful research/ historical evidence; it can show us things not found anywhere else. Not very: it was built much later; it might not be accurate in every detail. [3]
    c) Any two from: smoky – no chimney; cold in winter – no glass in windows; crowded – only one or two rooms; smelly – a third of the floor space was penned off for animals that lived inside. [2]

11. Around 1.5 million [1]
12. They were given a small plot of land to work for themselves [1]; in return they had to work for their landowner when required [1]; this might be four or five days a week. [1]
13. The king [1]
14. a) One quarter [1]
    b) Barons [1]; and bishops [1]
15. Feudal system [1]
16. The feudal system controlled the people by giving out land in return for loyalty [1]; everyone had to be loyal to the group above them and this kept people under the control of their lord. [1]

Pages 8–9 Christendom and the Crusades

1. Latin [1]
2. Any three from: Latin was the language of educated people and a common language throughout Europe; church services were Catholic and all Catholic services were in Latin; gave the services an air of mystery; every priest throughout the Church spoke Latin. [3]
3. Any four from: the king/rich people gave the Church money and land; people wanted to praise God; people hoped their donations would help them get to heaven when they died; there was only one Catholic Church; few people other than Church people could read and write so priests and their scribes did important things for the king; everybody went to church often. [4]
4.
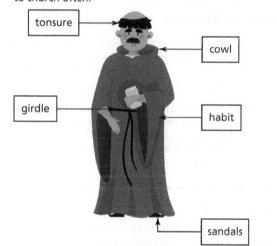
[5]
5. Any five from: pray; go to church seven times a day; care for the sick; work; grow food; copy books; keep records; tried to live according to their vow of poverty; tried to live according to their vow of chastity. [5]
6. Any two from: love of God; security; attracted to the life; want to help people; escape from home; career; to learn to read and write; some children were forced to become novices (trainee monks). [2]
7. Praying that the sick person recovered [1]; treating them with herbs and home-made medicines [1]; providing clean beds and clean water to aid recovery [1]; monasteries and nunneries were perhaps the only places ordinary people could get medical help. [1]
8. Any two from: monks provided education to some people; copying out books by hand so others could read them; keeping chronicles (history books) that recorded the main events of the time, e.g. the *Anglo-Saxon Chronicle*. [2]

Pages 10–11 Magna Carta

1. Chancellor [1]
2. Archbishop of Canterbury – the head of the Church in England [1]

3. Any three from: who has the most power in England – the king or the Pope; the right of Church people to be tried in Church courts; the fact that Becket had become very religious and took his job as Archbishop very seriously; Becket refused to make reforms to the Church courts as Henry wished; as Archbishop, Thomas felt he had to obey God not Henry. **[3]**
4. He was killed in Canterbury Cathedral **[1]** by four of Henry's knights. **[1]**
5. Any three from: he walked barefoot to Canterbury Cathedral; he allowed the monks to whip him; he spent a night praying at Becket's tomb; he sent the four knights on a pilgrimage to Jerusalem; he did not try to change the Church courts again. **[3]**
6. Any two from: King John is slumped at the table; surrounded by bishops and barons – John has no choice; the disapproving looks on the faces of the barons. **[2]**
7. Any three from: he lost lots of land in France and Ireland; he made them pay lots of taxes; law and order was breaking down; John was greedy. **[3]**
8. To make him stick to the rules for running the country. **[1]**
9. a) Any two from: he stayed king; avoided a civil war; allowed him time to rebuild his army; a temporary truce until he could defeat the barons; reduction in his power as king. **[2]**
   b) Any two from: it made John listen to them and their complaints; limited the king's power, showed John that there are rules even a king must stick to; set out the relationship between king and barons clearly; avoided civil war. **[2]**
   c) None whatsoever **[1]**; avoided a war that they would have had to fight in. **[1]**

Pages 12–13 The Black Death

1. The Black Death originated in **China** in 1347. From there it spread to the Black Sea. It was brought to Europe by **Italian** merchants. Slowly it spread across Europe, arriving in England, at the port of **Weymouth**, by early 1349. It spread across the whole country by the end of **1349**. As much as **30–45%** of the population died from the Black Death. **[1 mark per correct answer, up to 6 marks]**
2. Any two from: buboes, or swellings, all over their bodies; priest praying over them, praying/asking for forgiveness from the priest or Church was seen as a good way to try and save yourself; the image was in a Bible and people believed God had sent the plague as a punishment. **[2]**
3. Any two from: flagellants moved in procession; prayed to God for forgiveness of their sins; cutting up a pigeon and rubbing it over the infected part of your body; drinking vinegar; eating arsenic; rubbing chopped up onions and/ or herbs on the buboes; trying to pop the buboes; drying a frog out in the sun and then putting it on the buboe to suck out the poison; sitting near a fire or in a sewer to drive out the fever. **[2]**
4. a) Any three from: empty churches; deserted villages; high prices; buildings were in disrepair/collapsed; workers could ask for higher rates of pay; workers could refuse to work for low wages; landowners faced a loss of crops if they were not prepared to pay workers properly; shortage of priests; many people had died. **[3]**
   b) Empty churches **[1]**, because he was a priest. **[1]**
   c) Could be any of his points, for example: 'all foodstuffs became dear'; 'many villages were completely deserted'. There is no right or wrong answer here – it is a matter of opinion and emphasis. State a consequence **[1]**, then give a reason for your choice. **[1]**
   d) 1 mark will be awarded for stating what you think the most important consequence of the Black Death was **[1]**; 2 further marks will be given for two reasons stated in support of your choice of most important consequence. **[2] [Maximum of 3 marks available]**

Pages 14–15 The Peasants' Revolt

1. Any three from: the Poll Taxes of 1377, 1379 and 1381 – most ordinary people thought these were unfair **[1]**; disputes between landlords and villagers – many landlords increased rents even though there had been many bad harvests **[1]**; Statute of Labourers, 1351; impact of the Black Death on work, prices, etc. **[3]**
2. Skilled workers **[1]**; Better-off farm workers **[1]**
3. Not at all – the King sent the peasants home **[1]**; the leaders of the rebellion were tracked down and killed **[1]**; the aims of the revolt were not achieved. **[1]**
4. Possible answers: Not very **[1]**: because he was killed/ the revolt failed. **[1]** Quite **[1]**: because his speeches and sermons inspired the revolt. **[1]** Very **[1]**: because he was one of the key leaders **[1]**; his ideas inspired the peasants. **[1]** **[1 mark for each point made, up to a maximum of 5 marks]**
5. Possible answers: Wat Tyler **[1]**: because he kept his huge army together **[1]**; put real pressure on the King and rulers. **[1]** Richard II **[1]**: because he kept his nerve **[1]**; promised to do as they asked – then changed his mind and killed any leaders he could lay his hands on – restored law and order. **[1] [1 mark for each point made, up to a maximum of 5 marks]**

Pages 16–17 Progress Test 1

1. Riot/revolt **[1]**
2. Harold; William I; Henry II; John; Richard II **[5]**
3. Life of chastity; Life of prayer **[2]**
4. The Church was rich – people kept giving it land and money **[1]**; few people other than Church leaders could read and write **[1]**; everyone went to church. **[1]**
5. Rich – a lot **[1]**, most Anglo-Saxon rulers and landowners replaced by Normans **[1]**; Poor – not a lot **[1]**, still had to work long hours and had a landlord controlling their life **[1]**, very little income. **[1]**
6. Any – supported by any relevant points **[3 marks]** and reaching a conclusion – based on evidence **[2 marks]**. Example: William, as he had not one but two heirs **[1]**; any revolts were quickly put down **[1]**; no one invaded England after 1067 Viking raid failed **[1]**; he gave lots of land and wealth to the Church/many of his leading officials were churchmen, close relationship with the Pope **[1]**; but people could only get a fair trial if they were a Norman, not a Saxon. **[1]**
7. Example answer; disease, e.g. the Black Death **[1]**; heavy taxes – the Poll Taxes leading to the Peasants' Revolt **[1]**; famine and food shortages – the 14th century was particularly bad **[1]**; harsh laws – you could be hanged if caught poaching the king's deer. **[1]**

Britain 1509–1745

Pages 18–19 Reformation and Counter Reformation

1. Mostly to do with the need for a male heir. **[1]**
2. Henry needed a male heir but he and his wife, Catherine of Aragon, had a daughter, Mary, and no sons, and Catherine was too old to have more children **[1]**; the head of the Church, the Pope, who lived in Rome, had to agree to the divorce, and he would not do this. **[1]**
3. 1534 **[1]**
4. The need for a divorce so Henry could have a son with a different wife **[1]**; dispute over who runs the Church – the king or the Pope **[1]**; money – Henry was very short of money so resented the Church being so rich. **[1]**
5. Any three from: monasteries owned 25% of all farmland; monks were said to be living too well and not keeping their vows of chastity and poverty; the Church was too powerful; he wanted the Church's land to sell it to his friends; he wanted the wealth of the monasteries for himself. **[3]**

6.   Any three from: the Bible was written in English; the
     service was in English; the inside of the church was much
     simpler; priests wore simple robes; Catholic bishops were
     imprisoned. [3]
7.   a) John Rogers is being burned at the stake. [1]
     b) Any two from 'Yes' or 'No' or a combination: Yes: he
         was writing just after the death of Queen Mary; he was
         alive at the time; he refused to go to Catholic services.
         No: he didn't actually see John Rogers being burned –
         he was exiled in Europe at the time; it is propaganda –
         he hated Catholics and Queen Mary. [2]
8.   Any four from 'Yes' or 'No' or a combination: Yes: over
     280 Protestants were burned while she was queen; over
     800 rich Protestants fled to live in exile in Europe; the
     Pope became the head of the Church again; she did not
     allow any opposition to her religious views. No: Henry
     VIII executed many more religious dissenters; Edward VI
     and Elizabeth I also executed religious dissenters – Mary
     was no worse than the others. [Your answer must reach a
     conclusion to gain full marks] [4]

Pages 20–21 Causes of the English Civil War

1.   1625 [1]
2.   This was the belief that God had chosen the monarch; this
     meant that the monarch only had to answer to God, not to
     people on Earth (his/her subjects). [1]
3.   a) Charles married a Catholic – people thought he would
         make the country Catholic again [1]; the new Prayer
         Book was very unpopular. [1]
     b) Any two from: Charles spent lots of money and was
         always short of money; Charles kept asking Parliament
         for more money and when they refused he closed
         Parliament down; he introduced unpopular taxes, e.g.
         Ship Money. Ship Money was meant to be raised in
         ports to pay for the Navy but Charles made everyone
         pay Ship Money. [2]
     c) Charles ruled without Parliament agreeing laws for 11
         years [1]; Parliament thought they should agree which
         taxes the King could raise/Parliament thought they
         should help the King rule the country. [1]
     d) **1 mark for choosing an answer and 1 mark for a
         conclusion.** Any of the answers to a)–c). Your answer
         must have a conclusion, e.g. power [1]; because neither
         side – King or Parliament – were prepared to give way
         over who should run the country. [1]
4.   a) To protect the musketeers. [1]
     b) To kill as many enemy soldiers as they could. [1]
     c) To smash through the enemy lines. [1]
5.   Any four from: full-time professional soldiers; could be
     asked to serve anywhere in the country; officers could
     not be Members of Parliament – they, too, were full-time
     soldiers; many recruits were Puritans or had very strong
     religious views; promoted on merit rather than hereditary
     title/status; had to abide by strict rules; well trained. [4]
6.   Any three from: elections to Parliament every two years;
     freedom of religious views; the law should apply equally to
     everyone – rich and poor alike; Parliament should run the
     country, not the king; every man should have a vote. [3]

Pages 22–25 The Interregnum

1.   1649 [1]
2.   No king to rule the country – Parliament ruled the country
     until 1653, when Cromwell became Lord Protector. [1]
3.   Any five from: peace/the Civil War ended; Puritans in
     charge who believed in hard work and prayer; theatres
     closed; swearing banned; inns and alehouses limited;
     dancing, bear-baiting and most sports – except archery –
     banned; Christmas and Easter celebrations prohibited; taxes
     went up; women were banned from wearing make-up. [5]

4.   Better-off: peace [1]; restore law and order [1]; no king. [1]
     Worse-off: any three from: rule by Puritans was rather dull;
     taxes went up; Parliament found it hard to agree what to
     do next; ordinary people still had no say in government –
     some people wondered what all the fighting had
     been for. [3]
5.   a)

	Charles I	Cromwell
Was born to rule	x	
Believed Parliament should run the country		x
Was a great general of the army		x
Was indecisive – found it hard to make up his mind	x	x
Wasn't very good at making speeches	x	
Was a Puritan		x
Married a Catholic	x	
Died in his own bed		x

[8]

     b) Example answer, any three from: Charles – he was the
         major cause of the Civil War because he refused to
         compromise with Parliament; because of the Divine
         Right of Kings; because of his Catholic wife; because he
         spent so much money. [3]
6.   Charles I's son, also called Charles, who had been living in
     exile in Europe – he became Charles II. [1]
7.   1660 [1]
8.   The Merry Monarch [1]
9.   More than 12 [1]
10. He restored the lands and wealth of all those who had lost
     these things under Cromwell [1]; he had Cromwell's body
     dug up, put on trial, found guilty of regicide and hung
     from the gallows at Tyburn [1]; 13 other people involved
     in Charles I's execution were put on trial, found guilty and
     hanged. [1]
11. The Church of England was restored [1]; no other church
     services were allowed [1]; you couldn't become an MP,
     teacher or priest unless you belonged to the Church of
     England. [1]
12. Any one from: easy going; reopened theatres, etc.; his court
     was very happy, jolly, riotous; relief at a return to normality;
     end of the chaos of 1658–60. [1]
13. Any three from: Very: he was there; he saw what
     happened; he recorded what he did and what he saw; but
     it is only his views/experiences/ideas. [3]
14. a) Either – it's the reasons given about the usefulness of
         the *Diary* extract that matter. Example answer: Source
         B tells us about the impact of the plague [1]; how
         there was no-one left to treat the sick [1]; how sick
         people were roaming the streets, suggesting there was
         nowhere for them to be treated. [1]
     b) Either – it's the reasons given about the usefulness of
         the *Diary* extract that matter. Example answer, any
         three from: Source A tells us that Pepys liked to see
         things for himself; to be at important events; he was
         curious; he liked to be seen at major events; he was a
         royalist as Major-General Harrison had been a leading
         figure under Cromwell and at the trial of Charles I. [3]
15. Pepys's eyesight began to fail, so he couldn't see to
     write well. [1]

Pages 26–29 Progress Test 2

1.   1642 [1]
2.   Up to 30–45% [1]

3. Any three from: Marston Moor; Edgehill; Naseby; Newbury; Cheriton; Lostwithiel; Cropready Bridge; Nantwich; Chester. **[3]**
4. 1649 **[1]**
5.

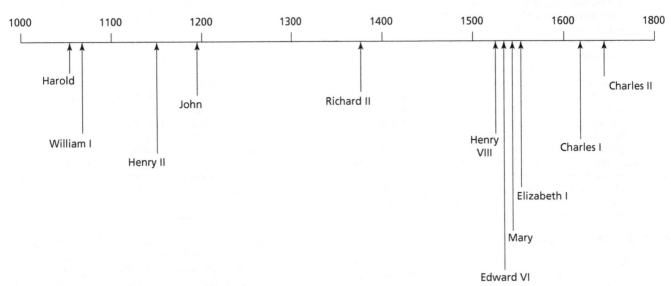

pike

pot helmet

leather snapsack containing food and spare clothes

iron breastplate or leather corselet

wool stockings

woollen breeches

[1 mark per correct answer, up to 6 marks]
6. Corrupt – not sticking to the rules **[1]**; people had new ideas about the part the Church should play in everyday life **[1]**; Protestants wanted change, Catholics wanted things to stay the same **[1]**; disputes over power – who should be more important – the king or the Pope. **[1]**
7. Producing a male heir **[1]**
8. Any choice of king is suitable as long as it is supported by evidence, and your answer must reach a conclusion, e.g. any three from: William – he conquered England; made the Church powerful; made England peaceful; put down any rebellions. **[3]**
9. Canterbury Cathedral **[1]**
10. The Peasants' Revolt **[1]**
11.

12. Very similar – dispute over who runs the country **[1]**; how to deal with a king who is not abiding by the rules. **[1]** Not very similar – John agreed Magna Carta with the barons **[1]**; Charles ended up fighting Parliament. **[1]** In conclusion … [you must supply a conclusion to gain the mark]. **[1]**
13. Latin **[1]**
14. Henry Knighton was a priest who lived near Leicester and died in 1396. **[1]** He wrote about the effects of the Black Death on the towns and villages of England. **[1]**
15. Flagellants moved in procession, whipping themselves, praying to God for the forgiveness of their sins. **[1]**
16. 'Between kings' **[1]**

Britain 1745–1901

Pages 30–31 British Transatlantic Slave Trade

1. 1619 **[1]**
2. Growing and harvesting cotton and sugar needed a large labour force **[1]**; most Native Americans had died of maltreatment and European diseases such as smallpox **[1]**; many slaves died due to brutal treatment, and so had to be frequently replaced with more slave labour. **[1]**
3. Any two from: as inferior to Europeans; uncivilised; in need of European rule/guidance; heathen; as physically stronger. **[2]**
4. a) Africans being marched off to a life of slavery **[1]**; how some Africans treated other Africans. **[1]**
    b) Very useful: it dates from Victorian times **[1]**; it shows us exactly what happened **[1]** it supports other evidence we have. **[1]** Not very useful: it does not show European slavers, so it is not representative of who dominated the slave trade **[1]**; it was made after slavery was abolished in Britain **[1]**; it is an artist's impression of only one event during the slave trade. **[1]** **[Any two points for a maximum of 2 marks]**
5. Any two from: he spent 60 years campaigning; travelled the whole country speaking against the trade; persuaded MPs to keep raising the topic in Parliament; brilliant at organising and publicity; displayed examples of equipment

| 1000 | 1100 | 1200 | 1300 | 1400 | 1500 | 1600 | 1800 |

Harold

Charles II

John

Richard II

William I

Henry VIII

Charles I

Henry II

Elizabeth I

Mary

Edward VI

[1 mark per correct answer, up to 11 marks]

used on slave ships (handcuffs, thumb screws etc.) as visual aids to show people the horrors of the slave trade; wrote a book on the abolition of the slave trade. **[2]**

6. 1807 **[1]**
7. Any two from: much of Britain's wealth depended on the slave trade; powerful people owned slaves and plantations in the Americas; it was thought that the government should not interfere in people's affairs. **[2]**
8. Any two from: he was an ex-slave who had bought his freedom and he wrote of his experiences; his autobiography was a bestseller and made people aware of the horrors of slavery; he showed people that black people were not the uncivilised/inferior people the slavers said they were. **[2]**
9. Either or both – there is no correct answer, but you must reach a conclusion. Example answers: Clarkson, any three of: because he spent his whole life campaigning; had influential friends; raised awareness; changed attitudes. **[3]** Equiano, because he had been a slave **[1]**; his personal experiences persuaded people **[1]**; he really knew what he was talking about. **[1]** Both – one could not have done it without the other **[1]**, and lots of other people too, e.g. Wilberforce, Sharp **[1]**; ordinary people who boycotted sugar, etc. **[1]**

Pages 32–35 Britain as the First Industrial Nation

1. Wig-maker **[1]**
2. 1771 **[1]**
3. Plenty of water to power his machinery **[1]**; far away from the domestic workers in/around Manchester. **[1]**
4. a)

[Two correct labels for 1 mark, maximum of 2 marks available]
    b) Any one from: tv aerials; flower pots outside. **[1]**
    c) Any two from: it was where the hand-loom weavers worked – his factory was for spinning machines only; and he still needed domestic workers to weave his yarn into cloth; they needed as much light as possible to complete their work. **[2]**
5. At first he used packhorses, then he built the Cromford Canal. **[1]**
6. Any five from: grew fast, so no planning regulations, leading to slum housing/squalid conditions; poor transport meant people had to live near their work; government was reluctant to act to make things better; few toilets; poor water, meaning disease spread quickly; overcrowded houses – housing not built as quickly as the population increased. **[5]**
7. Disease was spread by bad air **[1]**; so to reduce disease you had to improve air quality. **[1]**
8. Either or both, or any combination. You must reach a conclusion. Example answers: Very: both aimed to deal with sewers **[1]**; rubbish collection **[1]**; provide clean water **[1]**; appoint a Medical Officer of Health. **[1]** Not very:

1848 encouraged local councils to act **[1]**; 1875 made it compulsory for local councils to act and do more things. **[1]** Conclusion: 1875 was a watershed – government at last insists on improving conditions in the cities. **[1] [Any two points + a conclusion for a maximum of 3 marks]**

9. a) Work at a machine **[1]**
    b) 2 shillings [10p] per week **[1]**
    c) 6 shillings and 3 pence [32p] per week **[1]**
10. Any two from: he became a cripple; he couldn't work his machine; he had to give up work; he got no compensation. **[2]**
11. Any two from: needed work; no other work available; no unemployment pay or sick pay – had to work. **[2]**
12.

Factory Act	Improvement made
1819 Cotton Mills and Factories Act	Limited the hours children could work in factories and introduced the first factory inspectors
1833 Factory Act	Limited the hours women and children could work to 10 hours a day
1847 Factory Act	Children under nine were not allowed to work in factories, and children aged 9–16 could only work for 12 hours per day

[3]

13. Any two from: trade – an empire was a strong market for exports, and a good source of the raw materials you needed to import; power – a big empire meant you controlled lots of countries and lots of people, making you very important; religion – Europeans thought it was important to spread Christianity. **[2]**
14. Britain **[1]**
15.

C – Canada: wheat; N – Nigeria: palm oil; E – Egypt: cotton; I – India: tea; A – Australia: wool; New – New Zealand: lamb
[6 marks available, must get each pair of answers correct for each mark]

16. 25% **[1]**

Pages 36–37 Democratic Reform

1. Be male **[1]**; own property **[1]**; live in certain areas. **[1]**
2. More men could vote **[1]**; some rotten boroughs [parliamentary seats controlled by a very few voters, such as Old Sarum or Dunwich] were abolished **[1]**; some new cities now had an MP, e.g. Manchester. **[1]**
3. A mass movement set up after the 1832 Act to demand more reforms **[1]**; wanted all men to have the vote. **[1]**
4. Any two from: refused to discuss them; put Chartist leaders in prison; said there would be no more reform ever. **[2]**
5. More men – middle class and skilled workers – could vote **[1]**; men renting property [not owning it] could now vote. **[1]**

6. Secret ballot – nobody knew how you voted **[1]**; which reduced bribery and threats from rich people. **[1]**
7. Two-thirds of all men could now vote **[1]**; still no women could vote. **[1]**
8. One – secret ballot **[1]**
9. Either or both, or any combination. Example answers: Not at all: not all men/no women could vote **[1]**; you still needed to be rich to be an unpaid MP **[1]**; government still run only by rich men. **[1]** More than it was: 6 million men could now vote **[1]**; there was the secret ballot to reduce corruption and threats **[1]**; rulers were now listening more to the demands of ordinary people. **[1]** **[Any three points for a maximum of 3 marks]**

Pages 38–41 Progress Test 3

1. King William – he had absolute power **[1]**. Any two from: each of the others lost power to other groups in society, e.g. – King John to the barons **[1]**; Richard to the peasants, although he got it back **[1]**; King Charles I to Parliament **[1]**; by 1884 when most men could vote Victoria could influence the government but not force it to do something. **[1]**
2. For the first time government insisted that councils acted to improve public health **[1]**; government took responsibility for improving peoples' lives. **[1]**
3. 1833 **[1]**
4. a) 250,000 **[1]**
   b) 500,000 **[1]**
5. Railways **[1]**
6. Women **[1]**; unskilled working men **[1]**
7. 12 million **[1]**
8. a) You can choose any one change. **[1]**
   b) You can choose any logical order. **[3]**
   c) Any choice is acceptable, use PEE in your answer, e.g. P – industry, not agriculture, made the country much richer; E – more jobs/technology; E – increased the wealth of the country as individuals became better paid in due course. **[Any three points for a maximum of 3 marks]**
9. 1875 **[1]**
10. a) 6 million **[1]**
    b) Zero **[1]**
11.

12. In 1865 [by the 13th Amendment] **[1]**
13. Protestant **[1]**
14. Your answer could be any of these Acts, then supply three supporting details for the Act you have chosen, e.g. 1884 **[1]**; because by now 66% of men could vote **[1]**; constituencies were fairer **[1]**; ordinary people were being listened to. **[1]**
15. a) Harold Godwinson **[1]**
    b) Battle of Hastings, October 1066 **[1]**
16. Either or both, or any combination. You must reach a conclusion. Example answers: Very: lots of people died **[1]**; no-one really understood the causes. **[1]** Not very: plague was spread by fleas, cholera by dirty water **[1]**; John Snow discovered the cause of cholera in 1854, it took until the 19th century for scientists to understand how the plague spread. **[1]** In conclusion, I think ----------. **[1]** **[Any four points + a conclusion for a maximum of 5 marks]**
17. Steam power **[1]**

Britain 1901–Present

Pages 42–43 Women's Suffrage

1. Because the husband made all the important decisions **[1]**; and was supposed to look after their wife's interests. **[1]**
2. Any two from: control her own money and property once they got married; get a divorce unless her husband deserted her or beat her; leave her husband's home and live somewhere else without his permission. **[2]**
3. a) Looking after the home and the children. **[1]**
   b) Any two from: many women, for different reasons, had to work to feed the family; women who felt restricted by the narrow boundaries that had been set for their lives, and wished to work or seek further education; unmarried wealthier women who had no income also had to work but found it hard to get suitable jobs. **[2]**
4. Right to keep their own property when they married **[1]**; Right to keep their own income when they married **[1]**
5. National Union of Women's Suffrage Societies (NUWSS) **[1]**

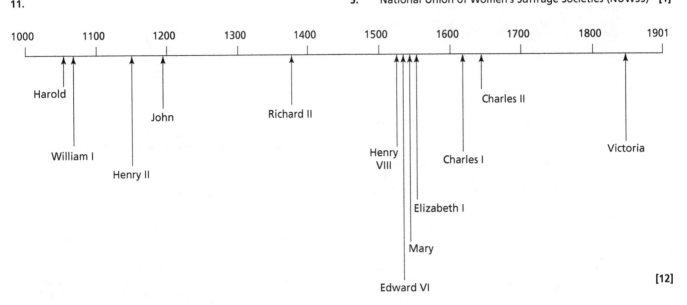

[12]

6. Millicent Fawcett [1]
7. Emmeline Pankhurst [1]
8.

Tactics	NUWSS	WSPU
Had a slogan, 'Deeds not Words'		x
Wanted only richer women who owned property to have the vote	x	
Used peaceful, persuasive tactics in an attempt to persuade MPs to give them the vote	x	
Used violent methods, such as putting bombs in post boxes and breaking windows, to publicise the issue of women's suffrage		x
Disrupted political meetings to get publicity		x

[1 mark for each correct point up to a maximum of 5 marks]

9. a) 'Yes' or 'No' is acceptable but a reason must be given, e.g. Yes – the historian has researched it; No – the historian was not there. [1]
   b) Yes – in 1918 not all women could vote [1]; women were still paid much less than men [1]; women were still expected to work and look after the home. [1] No – there had been changes for some women in the 1870s and 1880s [1]; women over 30 who owned property could now vote [1]; women thought having the vote would improve their lives – at least they would have a say in making the laws. [1] **[Any two points for a maximum of 2 marks]**

Pages 44–47 The First World War

1.

Allied powers	Central powers
Russia	Germany
France	Austria-Hungary
Great Britain	

[1 mark for each correct country up to a maximum of 5 marks]

2. Yes: the main powers had colonies all around the world [1]; this meant the fighting spread to South America, Africa and Asia [1]; troops were brought to Europe from the colonies to fight, e.g. thousands of Indian troops fought for the British in France in 1914. [1]

3. Any two from: men went off to fight, women had to do the men's work; German submarines sinking merchant ships, led to food shortages; air attacks by Zeppelins and, later, bombers; Defence of the Realm Act affected peoples' everyday lives. [2]

4. a) Groups of friends/workers/men from the same street, town or factory who joined the army to fight together. [1]
   b) Encouraged people to volunteer – could join up with people you know. [1]
   c) There might be lots of casualties from the same street, factory or town, which would damage morale. [1]

5. a) They are wearing kilts and playing bagpipes. [1]
   b) Either or both views can be given. Any three from: Very: barbed wire; explosions; tin helmets; dead men; trenches. Not very: no mud; no shell holes; not much barbed wire. [3]
   c) Any three from: Useful; it is from the time; it shows the fighting; shows soldiers going 'over the top'; shows artillery; shows no-man's land; it is of an actual battle. Less useful; it is an artist's drawing – he wasn't there; soldiers weren't always fighting, they had to live in the trenches too; it is made to look heroic to people at home in Britain (so had a propaganda purpose). [3]

6. a) A tank [1]
   b) They could cross no-man's land using the tank as cover [1]; it could destroy German barbed wire and machine gun posts. [1]
   c) It would attract artillery shells from German guns [1]; it was not very reliable at first and could easily break down, leaving soldiers exposed to danger. [1]

7. Examples of acceptable answers:

New weapon	Impact
Gas	Could knock out or kill the enemy without risk to your own side (unless the wind changed)
Machine guns	Could fire up to 600 rounds a minute, making it very dangerous to attack enemy trenches
Aircraft	Could spot enemy troops and direct attacks at them; could drop bombs on enemy trenches

[1 mark for each correct point up to a maximum of 3 marks]

8. Any of the three, with at least two supporting facts. Example answer: Tank, because it made it much easier to get across no-man's land and successfully attack enemy trenches [1]; at first there was no effective way to stop tanks. [1]

9. The Treaty of Versailles [1]

10. Any four from: Germany took blame for the war [Article 231, War Guilt Clause]; had to pay reparations of £6,600 million to pay for damage caused by the fighting; German army was reduced to 100,000 men [no conscription]; Germany lost lots of its land, both at home and across its empire, to other countries; no air force allowed; no submarines allowed; only six battleships allowed. [4]

11. a) Two [Fred Garrill and John William Ward] [1]
    b) Suvla Bay [Gallipoli campaign] [1]; Ypres [France and Belgium] [1]
    c) Either or both views can be given. Any two from: Very useful – it tells us who from the village died; where they were killed; that the people of the chapel chose to remember them; memorials like this can be found all over Britain, we can assume that because of this these memorials show that the war had a wide-reaching cost to almost all British villages, towns and cities. Not very useful – it is just one small village; only two men; doesn't tell us about elsewhere in Britain. [2]

Pages 48–51 The Second World War

1. In 1933, **Adolf Hitler** came to power in Germany. He was determined to make Germany a **great power** again by tearing up the **Treaty of Versailles** and building up Germany's **army**. In 1938 he took over **Austria** and **the Sudetenland** [which was part of Czechoslovakia]. No country was prepared to stand up to him. This policy was called **appeasement**. **[1 mark per correct answer, up to 7 marks]**

2. 1939 [1]

3. Any two from: Hitler made promises but did not keep them; no other leader believed Hitler would fight a war; Hitler saw the other leaders as weak and continued to push for more. [2]

4. 1: Evacuation of children from the cities and towns; 2: Battle of Britain; 3: Blitz; 4: V1 and V2 rockets attack Britain; 5: VE Day **[1 mark per correct answer, up to 5 marks]**

5. a) People are farming/vegetable gardening. [1]
   b) All the young men and women were conscripted to fight or do essential war work. [1]
   c) Either or both views can be given. Any three from: Very useful – primary evidence from the time; shows how important it was for everyone to help; how necessary it was to grow all the food we could. Not very useful – it is only one piece of evidence – we need more; it only shows 1943, not the other years. [3]

6.

Battle	Month/year	Significant event
Midway	June 1942	US troops stop the Japanese advance in the Pacific
El Alamein	October–November 1942	Britain and her allies stop the German advance in North Africa
Stalingrad	August 1942–February 1943	Russian troops stop German advance into the Soviet Union
Atlantic	1943–44	American and British navies stop German submarines sinking supply ships
D-Day	June 1944	British, American and Canadian troops land in Europe and begin to recapture France

[1 mark for each correct month/year/significant event up to a maximum of 10 marks]

7. **a)** A German submarine has sunk a ship taking supplies to Britain. **[1]**
b) Any one from: vital supplies – food, ammunition, goods – came by sea to keep the war effort going; submarines were sinking lots of these ships. **[1]**
8. Hitler committed suicide. **[1]**
9. Victory in Europe **[1]**
10. The atomic bomb **[1]**
11. Source A (the photograph) shows the destruction/impact of the bomb **[1]**; Source B (the historian) tells us why the bomb was used (explains why Truman thought it was a good idea to drop the bomb)/there are other reasons why the bomb was dropped – to frighten Russia, because the USA had the bomb – that might explain why it was dropped. **[1]**
12. 15 August 1945 [VJ Day] **[1]**

Pages 52–53 Creation of the Welfare State

1. 35% **[1]**
2. 28% **[1]**
3. Booth and Rowntree and others showed how bad things were for many people **[1]**; the Labour Party, a party of working people, was beginning to take votes away from the Liberal Party **[1]**; government ideas began to change – they began to accept responsibility for the lives of ordinary people and thought they could work to make their lives better. **[1]**
4. In childhood – so they grew up well **[1]**; in old age – when they could no longer work **[1]**; when sick or unemployed. **[1]**
5. Any two from: 1906 Free School Meals Act; 1907 School Medical Inspectors Act; 1908 Old Age Pensions Act; 1911 National Insurance Act; set up Labour Exchanges to help people find jobs. **[2]**
6. 1942 **[1]**
7.

'Giant'	Problems this caused
Want	People didn't earn enough money to live well and keep healthy …
Disease	People became sick and so could not work, so they didn't eat enough …
Squalor	Poor housing meant that people became sick, couldn't work …
Ignorance	Children were poorly educated, so didn't get a well-paid job; or didn't know the best way to spend their wages/cook properly …
Idleness	If you couldn't get a job, then you couldn't eat …

[1 mark for each correct answer up to a maximum of 5 marks]
8. Very similar **[1]**; a deprived childhood/unemployment/sickness ruined peoples' lives. **[1]**

9. Either, but more likely to say Labour post-1945 **[1]**; because they were more far-reaching – NHS aimed to help people 'from the cradle to the grave'. **[1]**

Pages 54–55 Britain's Place in the World 1945–Present

1. **a)** Any two from: Yes – rationing was ended; industry was growing; people were more optimistic. No – some people still didn't have jobs; people still lived in poor housing. **[2]**
b) It tells us what the Prime Minister thought – it is his opinion – he will want people to think he is doing a good job and so will tell people positive things **[1]**; he is trying to tell people they are better off **[1]**; it doesn't tell us what anyone else thought. **[1]**
2. Any two from: 1979, thousands of workers on strike; protesting about limiting pay rises to 5% when inflation was 20%+; led to defeat of Labour Government and election of Margaret Thatcher. **[2]**
3. Any two from: many traditional industries such as coal mining, iron smelting, shipbuilding, have closed down; huge increase in self-employment; technology and services, e.g. call centres employ many more people now. **[2]**
4. **a)** None of them **[1]**
b) Vacuum cleaner; washing machine; fridge; cooker. **[4]**
c) All of them **[1]**
5. **a)** 12 million **[1]**
b) Doubled, from 6 million **[1]**
6. Margaret Thatcher [in 1979] **[1]**
7. Choose any – looking for the impact on life. Example answers: The contraceptive pill: because it allowed women more control over when, or if, they had babies; as a result more women could work. The Internet: because of improved communication, allowing people to work from home; streaming films and tv shows; changed the way we interact with people. **[1 mark for each point up to 2 marks]**

Pages 56–57 Progress Test 4

1. Choose any – the reasons are the key. Example answer: medieval England – peasant, land to work; not much money but fairly safe; small population; monasteries to look after you if you were poorly/poor; government mostly left you alone. **[1 mark for each point up to 2 marks]**
2. Suffragettes **[1]**
3. King Harold **[1]**
4. The Blitz **[1]**
5. Liverpool and Manchester Railway [1830] **[1]**
6. Any choice is suitable as long as it is supported by evidence, and your answer must reach a conclusion. Very: lots of soldiers doing the fighting **[1]**; muskets (rifles) were the main weapons **[1]**; lots of soldiers died. **[1]** Not very: trench warfare **[1]**; new technology in First World War, e.g. tanks, gas, planes **[1]**; cavalry no longer any use in war – replaced by tanks **[1]**; beginning of total war – rations and bombing towns and cities. **[1]** In conclusion, I think ……………………… **[1]** **[Any four points + a conclusion for a maximum of 5 marks]**
7. Any five from: NHS, free medical care; Family Allowance introduced for low-paid workers; implemented the Education Act, school leaving age raised to 15; nationalised major industries, better working conditions; more influence of trade unions in deciding wages and working conditions; built lots of new houses to replace those damaged in the Second World War. **[5]**
8. **a)** 47 million **[1]**
b) 58 million **[1]**
c) 67 million **[1]**
d) Any two from: better healthcare; higher wages mean better food and housing; more government intervention in the lives of ordinary people, helping to look after them. **[2]**
9. Harold Macmillan **[1]**

10. Harold; William I, Henry II, John; Richard II; Henry VIII, Edward VI, Mary, Elizabeth I; Charles I; Charles II; Victoria; Edward VII, George VI; Elizabeth II **[1 mark for each correct answer]** **[15]**
11. Armistice Day [in First World War] – the fighting stopped **[1]**
12. Six **[1]**
13. 1649 [after the execution of Charles I] until 1660 [the restoration of Charles II]. **[1]**
14. Wat Tyler **[1]**
15. Russia **[1]** v Germany and Austria-Hungary **[1]**
16. 1: Martin Luther and the Protestants; 2: Chartists; 3: Suffragettes **[3]**
17. a) 6 June 1944 **[1]**
    b) Allied invasion of France to liberate it from German occupation **[1]**; beginning of the end of the Second World War **[1]**; Allies needed to land in Europe to be able to defeat Hitler and Germany. **[1]**

British Social History

Pages 58–61 Migration To and From the British Isles

1. All 800 million people living in the Commonwealth **[1]**
2. Shortage of workers **[1]**; not many people wanted to do the low-skilled, low-paid jobs. **[1]**
3. a) £28 **[1]**
   b) A troopship **[1]**; the cheapest accommodation was on the troopdeck. **[1]**
   c) Very basic/cheap and cheerful **[1]**
4. Very poor housing **[1]**; discrimination – many landlords did not want to rent houses to migrants from the Caribbean [or Ireland] **[1]**; even very skilled workers could only get low-paid unskilled jobs. **[1]**
5.

Reason to migrate	Push factor	Pull factor
War	x	
Better education		x
Poverty	x	
Better standard of living		x
Lack of opportunity in native country	x	

[1 mark for each correct answer up to a maximum of 5 marks]

6. Any two from: India; Pakistan; Bangladesh; East Africa. **[2]**
7. Europe **[1]**; e.g. any one from: Poland, Latvia, Lithuania; Romania. **[1]**
8. Any two from: multicultural society; eating habits, e.g. curry, pizza; musical influences, e.g. reggae; fashion influences, e.g. Indian clothes; religion, e.g. Islam, non-Anglican Christianity; food shops, e.g. selling different types of food; more NHS workers; any other relevant point. **[2]**
9. Any sensible suggestion – there is no correct answer. **[1 mark for each sensible suggestion up to a maximum of 3 marks]**
10. Enoch Powell [a Conservative MP] **[1]**
11. a) High: 1920s massive unemployment after World War I **[1]**; High: 1930s massive unemployment in the Great Depression **[1]**; Low: 1940s the world was at war. **[1]**
    b) Any four from: Canada; Australia; New Zealand; South Africa; Kenya; [then] Rhodesia [now Zimbabwe]. **[4]**
12. £10 **[1]**

13. Most immigrants appeared to be different, e.g. appearance/behaviour/culture/traditions **[1]**; immigrants often concentrated in small areas, close together, making some British people feel threatened. **[1]**
14. Some people thought that the 'best' people were leaving the country – young, skilled, clever **[1]**; it would be hard for Britain to become richer/the economy get stronger if too many people went to live in other countries. **[1]**
15.

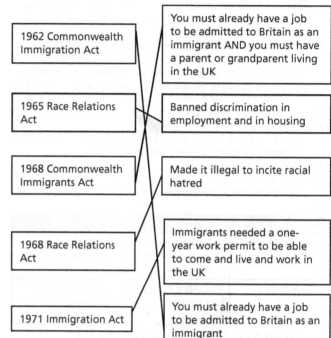

[1 mark for each correct answer up to a maximum of 5 marks]

16. Any two from: Yes: laws were passed to make life better/ discrimination was banned. No: just because laws were passed doesn't mean that life was fairer – immigrants still had low-paid jobs; poorer housing; suffered from discrimination. **[2]**

World History

Pages 62–65 USA in the 20th Century

1. Any three from: cars; electricity; fridges; freezers; radios; telephones; cinema. **[3]**
2. Farming **[1]**; old industries, e.g. coal **[1]**
3. Credit – hire purchase/monthly payment plan **[1]**
4. The Ku Klux Klan **[1]**
5. a) Primary **[1]**
   b) Either or both, or any combination. Example answers: Very – it shows us that people had cars **[1]**; he is obviously proud of his car, having his photo taken at the wheel. **[1]** Not very – it is only one man and his car **[1]**; we don't know exactly where it is. **[1]** **[Any two points for a maximum of 2 marks]**
6. a) Wall Street Crash **[1]**
   b) America had loaned lots of money to Germany and now it wanted that money back. **[1]**
   c) No **[1]**; farmers and African-Americans are examples of people who didn't share in the wealth of the USA in the 1920s. **[1]**
7. 12 million **[1]**
8. 5,000 **[1]**

9. a) Primary [1]
   b) Yes – people are working [1]; No – it is California, not everywhere in the USA [1]; they are picking carrots by hand, which is low-paid temporary work. [1]
10. The USA didn't want Communism to spread any further in Asia [the Domino Theory]. [1]
11. 1964 [1]
12. American Air Force killing off the jungle by spraying it with chemical weapons [1]; with the aim of destroying the hiding places of North Vietnamese soldiers [called the Viet Cong] so that they could no longer carry out surprise attacks on US troops. [1]
13. The war was on TV/in the newspapers every day [1]; the army drafted young people to go and fight and many didn't want to go [1]; the war was expensive – taxes went up to pay for it [1]; thousands of American soldiers died [1]; it was the first war America lost. [1]
14. 1973 [Paris Peace Accords] [1]
15. Segregation [1]
16. Refused to give up her seat on a bus to a white person [1]; leading to the Montgomery Bus Boycott. [1]
17. Non-violent protest [1]
18. 250,000 [1]
19. An end to discrimination due to race/colour [1]
20.

Act	What it did
1964 Civil Rights Act	The government could force local towns, cities and states to end segregation in all public places, e.g. schools
1965 Voting Rights Act	This made it illegal to stop anyone who was entitled to vote from voting in elections

[1 mark for each correct answer up to 2 marks]
21. Very, any two from: important for his presence; his political contacts; his grassroots contacts; his inspiring speeches; his leadership. [2]

Pages 66–67 Progress Test 5

1. Many new industrial towns and cities now had MPs [1]; 'rotten' boroughs, which had no/few voters, were abolished [1]; more men who owned property could vote. [1]
2. Jamaica [1]
3. Any one from: war; poverty; unemployment; limited educational opportunities. [1]
4. Either choice/combination of choices is suitable, but your answer must reach a conclusion. Any two from: Very – lots of unemployment; old industries not making much money; struggling to get the economy going again. Not very – in the USA lots of government spending – the New Deal; the UK government was not spending money, cutting services. [2] You need to reach a conclusion to gain the third mark. [1]
5. Any one from: to find work; better education; more opportunity; better standard of living. [1]
6. Asia [1]
7. Any one from: children/mothers with babies from British cities; some disabled people; some teachers; some pregnant women. [1]
8. Emigration from Britain [1]
9. Anyone who wanted to drink alcohol had to break the law [1]; criminals made their own illegal alcohol/imported it and made lots of money so they became important and could bribe low-paid officials. [1]
10. Franklin D. Roosevelt [1]
11. Introduced the New Deal [1]. Any two from: spent lots of money to get people working [1]; talked up America so people felt more optimistic about the future [1]; tried to help the poorest people the most. [1]

12. Europe [1]
13. By fleas [1]
14. Worried about the spread of Communism [1]
15. London Transport [1]; the NHS [1]
16. Conscription – men aged between 19 and 25 were drafted into the US Army via a lottery and were sent to fight in Vietnam. [1]
17. More than ever before – the Civil Rights Act and the Voting Rights Act meant finally the government was acting [1]; still not completely – lower-paid jobs/live in worst areas. [1]
18. 1: English Civil War; 2: American War of Independence; 3: Crimean War; 4: The Great War; 5: Vietnam War [5]
19. King Henry II [1]
20. All women over the age of 21 [same basis as men] [1]
21. a) nun [1]
    b) nun; priest; bishop; archbishop [4]
22. Cromford [Derbyshire] [1]
23. a) Prohibition [1]
    b) Speakeasys [1]

Mixed Test-Style Questions

Pages 68–77 Mark Scheme

Marks are awarded as follows:
Simple, fragmentary answer: **1 mark**
Fuller answer with some description: **2–3 marks**
Full description and explanation, supported by evidence: **4–5 marks**

Page 68

For marks for these questions see the Mark Scheme
1. **One mark** for each valid observation (**5 marks** maximum). You might include the following observations.
   Useful:
   • It shows us that many people died.
   • It shows us that the Black Death didn't just affect England.
   Less useful:
   • It is from around 100 years after the Black Death came to England.
   • It shows dead people dancing, not the Black Death.
   • It doesn't help us understand how people thought, felt, and what they believed in 1349.
2. **One mark** for each valid observation (**5 marks** maximum). You might include the following observations.
   Useful:
   • It tells us what Richard II did.
   • It tells us that the rebels went home.
   Less useful:
   • It is just a tiny part of the story.
   • It doesn't tell us anything about the demands or actions of the peasants.
   • It doesn't tell us how Richard II punished the rebels once they left London – it was his violent actions then that really ended the revolt.

Page 70

For marks for these questions see the Mark Scheme
1. **One mark** for each valid observation (**5 marks** maximum). You might include the following observations.
   • Written by the Pope – Elizabeth's enemy – therefore she must be good!
   • 'She is only a woman' – tells us that female rulers were regarded as weak at the time.
   • Lists her enemies – all the major powers, including the Catholic Church – she was in trouble.

- Doesn't tell us anything about her problems inside England.
- Doesn't tell us about the issue of who she should marry, which was seen as a major problem by her subjects.

2. **One mark** for each valid observation (**5 marks** maximum). You might include the following observations.
    - He was a soldier – sword and hat.
    - He died aged 59.
    - He was regarded as very important by the Victorians – the statue was erected outside Parliament in 1899 – perhaps he was important to Parliament?
    - His statue was erected to commemorate the 300th anniversary of his birth.
    - There must be some controversy about his memory – it took 300 years for a statue of him to be erected outside Parliament.

Page 72

For marks for these questions see the Mark Scheme
1. **One mark** for each valid observation (**5 marks** maximum). You might include the following observations.
    - Speed – people could travel more quickly than at any other time before.
    - Safety – safer to travel by rail.
    - Communication – daily London newspapers reached the whole country the same day.
    - Time – everywhere in Britain had the same time – they used 'railway time'.
    - BUT in 1856 many places were not yet on the railway and still had to rely on turnpike roads/canals/walking.

2. **One mark** for each valid observation (**5 marks** maximum). You might include the following observations.
    - It tells us that poverty was a big problem – the workhouse is huge.
    - The wall suggests people were not supposed to enter – or leave – easily.
    - It doesn't tell us what it was like inside – what living conditions were like.
    - As a modern photograph and a tourist venue it is likely to be sanitised and more attractive than it was at the time – so it might give a misleading impression.
    - It can't tell us why workhouses were built or what Victorians thought about poor people.

Page 74

For marks for these questions see the Mark Scheme
1. **One mark** for each valid observation (**5 marks** maximum). You might include the following observations.
    - It shows a dugout for officers so it is bound to be more comfortable than a dugout for ordinary soldiers.
    - It shows just one part of the trench system – some parts were safer than others.
    - It is part of the French lines – it doesn't tell us about the British trenches.
    - It is heated, unlike most trenches – frostbite and exposure were very common.
    - It is obviously a posed photograph – would it be like this all the time?

2. **One mark** for each valid observation (**5 marks** maximum). You might include the following observations.
    - Britain depended on imports of food, weapons and raw materials so enemy submarines were a dangerous threat.
    - He was Prime Minister so he should know exactly what was going on.
    - At one stage in 1943 there was only 14 days of food left in Britain. Without more food Britain would have had to surrender to Germany.
    - Defeating the U-boats was a difficult problem that took well into 1943 to solve.

- There were other dangers that Churchill doesn't mention here, e.g. the threat of invasion, the Blitz.

Page 76

For marks for these questions see the Mark Scheme
1. **One mark** for each valid observation (**5 marks** maximum). You might include the following observations.
    - It is a cartoon from *Punch*, a satirical magazine, so we should be careful how we use it.
    - It is from 1954, so tells us how some people at the time felt about migration.
    - It helps us understand why people came to Britain from Jamaica, and what they left behind.
    - It helps us understand the difference in the climate – the way each figure is dressed.
    - It seems to suggest that some migrants are not very happy in Britain.

2. **One mark** for each valid observation (**5 marks** maximum). You might include the following observations.
    - It is only one historian's view – other historians might think differently.
    - Teenagers – music, clothes, social life all changed.
    - People were prepared to challenge old views and attitudes.
    - Women – the pill, legal abortion, work, home life all changed women's lives. At home, domestic appliances and ready meals allowed women more leisure time and also more time to go to work.
    - Definitely agree a social revolution began in the 1960s.

Pages 78–82 Mark Scheme

Marks are awarded as follows:
Simple, fragmentary answer: **1 mark**
Fuller answer with more description: **2–3 marks**
Full description with partial explanation: **4–5 marks**
Full description and explanation, supported by some evidence: **7–8 marks**
Full description and explanation, fully supported by evidence: **9–10 marks**

Page 78

For marks for these questions see the Mark Scheme.
1. Your answer might include the following reasons, backed up with explanations and facts:
    - William felt threatened by the Anglo-Saxons.
    - He needed to build safe places quickly.
    - He might have won the south, but he still didn't control the whole of England.
    - Enabled him to reward his nobles and give them land (start of the feudal system).
    Examples and facts to support this:
    - Early castles were made very quickly of wood – motte-and-bailey style.
    - They were built using forced labour, in response to a perceived threat to the Normans.
    - Later castles were made of stone – to control towns and cities, e.g. Exeter and Norwich.
    - Finally, some castles, e.g. the Tower of London, were built to impress upon the locals the fact that William was here to stay.

2. Your answer might include the following arguments, backed up with explanations and facts:
    - A bad son – he revolted against his father.
    - A bad brother – he tried to steal the throne from Richard I.
    - A bad king – upset both the Church and the barons; was known as 'Lackland' because he lost so much land in France.
    - A bad man – greedy, selfish, got very angry when people disagreed with him.
    But:
    - He improved the administration and finances of the country.

- The Tudors liked him because he stood up for the country against the Church.
- The Victorians liked him because he improved administration and government affairs.

In conclusion, I think........

3. Your answer might include the following arguments, backed up with explanations and facts:

Peasants' lives were secure because:
- Their lords gave them land.
- The Church looked after their spiritual and sickness needs.
- They didn't need much money.
- Their houses were cheap and easy to build.
- Farming was co-operative – families helped each other out with ploughs and oxen.

But:
- Bad harvests were common, and people could starve.
- Plague and disease often killed many people.
- They could not leave their villages without their lord's permission.
- They were frequently told what to do.
- Wars and raids, outlaws and bandits, often wrecked villages and crops.

In conclusion, I think........

Page 79

For marks for these questions see the Mark Scheme.

1. Your answer might include the following reasons, backed up with explanations and facts:
   - Dispute over who runs the country – king or Parliament?
   - Dispute over the direction of the Church – Puritans or Church of England?
   - Many people thought it was unnatural to fight against your king – who you had sworn an oath of loyalty to – even if he was a bad king.
   - All kinds of radical ideas emerged – such as those of the Levellers – that everyone was equal – or the idea that all men should vote.
   - Families were torn apart – often brother versus brother or father versus son/s.
   - The country's first professional army was used – the New Model Army.

2. Your answer might include the following reasons, backed up with explanations and facts:
   - The Catholic Church was seen to be corrupt – too wealthy and detached from ordinary people.
   - Many priests didn't carry out their duties very well.
   - The Church was a VERY important part of life.
   - New ideas – the Renaissance – emerged, and people began to question everything.
   - The Reformation meant that Protestants had different ideas about how to worship – in English; simple churches.
   - Different monarchs followed different forms of Christianity – Edward VI was strongly Protestant and wanted the country to be the same; Mary was a Catholic and tried to change the country back to that religion.
   - Monarchs used force to make people worship the way they demanded – many people resisted this.

3. Your answer might include the following reasons, backed up with explanations and facts:

Dislike of the Commonwealth:
- The point of getting rid of the King was so Parliament could rule – this did not happen during Cromwell's time as Lord Protector.
- Political uncertainty after the death of Cromwell.
- Inability to have a strong government that could make decisions.
- Many of Cromwell's decisions were unpopular.

Welcoming the new king:
- Most people supported the monarch.
- Charles was seen as having a rightful claim to the throne.
- Wanted to end uncertainty.

Page 80

For marks for these questions see the Mark Scheme.

1. Your answer might include the following reasons, backed up with explanations and facts:
   - The building – the glass prefabricated 'Crystal Palace'.
   - The contents – 100,000 exhibits – show off Britain's new economic strength and the riches of the Empire.
   - The contents – innovative goods from around the world.
   - The impact – 6 million visitors from all over the country. Special trains were run to transport people from all over Britain, cheap admission on some days.
   - The impact – profit of £186,000 – used to build museums and Royal Albert Hall in London.
   - Made Prince Albert's name.
   - Perfect symbol of Victorian Britain – Britain at its best.

2. Your answer might include the following reasons, backed up with explanations and facts:
   - Conditions in factories were usually bad – long hours, low wages, dangerous machinery, little inspection.
   - Conditions in the new industrial cities were very bad – poor housing squashed close together near the factories, bad health and water – government did little about it.
   - Some employers, like Titus Salt, did something about it – moved to Saltaire, built houses and a new factory – thought he would make more money if he treated his workers well.
   - Some others did the same – Cadbury Brothers – Bourneville; Lord Lever – Port Sunlight.
   - But most did not – until government regulations forced them to, most factories and living conditions were very bad.
   - In conclusion, Titus Salt was not typical.

3. Your answer might include the following reasons, backed up with explanations and facts:
   - Most people worked very long hours six days a week just to survive, so opportunities to enjoy entertainment were limited.
   - Travelling fairs came to town and provided opportunities for fun.
   - 1840s onwards many towns opened parks – public spaces – for recreation.
   - 1871 Bank Holidays introduced – four days of paid holiday for most workers.
   - Railways meant easier travel – going to the seaside.
   - Football, cricket and other sports grew.
   - Music hall and theatre were popular with better-off people.
   - By the 1900s more people had the money for leisure – magic lantern shows and early film became popular.

Page 81

For marks for these questions see the Mark Scheme.

1. Your answer might include the following reasons, backed up with explanations and facts:
   - The UK's first female Prime Minister.
   - Won the Falklands War against Argentina; defeated the coal miners' strike; weakened the power of the unions.
   - Sold off the nationalised industries and council houses – made life more competitive; re-focused Britain's economy.
   - Won three elections in a row, served continuously as Prime Minister for 11 years, from 1979–90.
   - Ditched by her party in 1990 when she was unpopular due to the Poll Tax she insisted on introducing.
   - A controversial figure – it depends on your point of view.

2. Your answer might include the following reasons, backed up with explanations and facts:
   - Yes: shortened the war; removed the need to invade Japan; saved the lives of many US troops; needed to know if the atom bomb – developed at great cost – really worked.

- No: Japan was already beaten; killed over 70,000 people immediately; destroyed most of the city; was used as a warning to Stalin and the USSR rather than to defeat Japan.
- In conclusion, I think......................
    because................................

3. Your answer might include the following reasons, backed up with explanations and facts:
    - Reasons for its introduction: evacuation and the impact of the war made people realise that the State needed to help look after people; impact of the Beveridge Report of 1942; a new Labour government – with a big majority – was elected in 1945 determined to make life better for ordinary people.
    - Aim: to provide support 'from the cradle to the grave' – health (NHS); money (Family Allowance); education (leaving age raised to 15).
    - Impact: life expectancy increased dramatically; some diseases, e.g. polio, eradicated; better education led to better work opportunities and wages (Macmillan and 'you've never had it so good').
    - But: more expensive than thought it would be, therefore charges had to be introduced for both prescriptions and spectacles.
    - In conclusion, I think it had a major/average/little impact on people's lives because…

Page 82

For marks for these questions see the Mark Scheme.
1. Your answer might include the following reasons, backed up with explanations and facts:
    - Growth of some industries, and better wages led to more demand for goods.
    - Refer to the production line (more goods made, very cheaply, which allowed more people to afford them).
    - But not all workers benefitted – African-Americans, farmers didn't benefit from the boom.
    - Lots of prosperity was based on borrowing, hire purchase and the stock market.
    - Stock market slumped, banks went bust – they had loaned too much money with not enough security; massive unemployment (12 million by 1932).
    - Business – over-production meant the market was saturated. Difficult international trade meant companies struggled to sell goods and therefore companies went bust. Workers were fired and this led to a rise in unemployment; fewer people could afford to buy goods … and the cycle continued.

- Very little government control and regulation – companies did what they wanted, not what was best for the country.
- No one really knew how to deal with the Great Depression.

2. Your answer might include the following reasons, backed up with explanations and facts:
    - Discrimination and segregation were widespread in the USA at this time.
    - Many people – white and African-American – protested against this, e.g. the Freedom Marches in the South; Rosa Parks and the Montgomery Bus Boycott in 1955.
    - Dr Martin Luther King was an extremely popular speaker, and respected for his views and contacts with politicians in Washington.
    - He was the main advocate of peaceful protest.
    - As a direct result of his 1963 Washington 'I have a Dream' speech, President Johnson passed the 1964 Civil Rights Act.
    - In conclusion, many people were important, but perhaps the most important was Dr Martin Luther King because he united the many voices and protests.

3. Your answer might include the following reasons, backed up with explanations and facts:
    - It wasn't originally unpopular – many Americans were happy to stop the spread of Communism – this was the time of the Cold War.
    - Most people, however, felt over time that this was not their battle to be fighting and many of the young soldiers sent did not know what they were fighting for.
    - Became more unpopular as the number of deaths of American soldiers rose.
    - The draft was extremely unpopular – and seemed to be unfair – college students were exempt, so it seemed the poor and African-Americans were more likely to be called up to fight. The average age of the US soldier was 19.
    - Every day on the television or in the newspapers, coverage of the war brought home the reality – images of atrocities being carried out (My Lai) by US soldiers were seen vividly in the homes of American citizens. It split the nation in two – it was the first major war to be on TV.
    - It increasingly seemed like a war the USA couldn't win, making it even more unpopular.
    - People realised that they weren't being told the truth by the government and army and turned against them and the war.

Acknowledgements

The author and publisher are grateful to the copyright holders for permission to use quoted materials and images.

P4 © Lebrecht Music & Arts/Alamy; P5 © IanDagnall Computing/Alamy; P15 © Florilegius/Alamy; P17: © INTERFOTO/Alamy; P19 © The History Collection/Alamy; P22 © Granger Historical Picture Archive/Alamy; P23 © The Picture Art Collection/Alamy; P25 © Ian Dagnall/Alamy; P27 © Classic Image/Alamy; P29 © FLPA/Alamy; P31 © World History Archive/Alamy; P36 © De Luan/Alamy; P44 Image used under Creative Commons license – The Geography of the Great War, by Frank M. McMurry, PH.D, 1919; P47 Photograph courtesy of Alf Wilkinson; P48 © Shawshots/Alamy; P52 © Pictorial Press Ltd/Alamy, © Heritage Image Partnership Ltd/Alamy; P58 © The Gleaner Company (Media) Limited; Table from *An introduction to Modern British History* 1900–1999 (2001) by Michael Lynch. Published by Hodder Education, © Keystone Press/Alamy; P65 © Everett Collection Inc/Alamy; P68 Wikimedia Commons; P76 © Punch Cartoon Library/TopFoto

All other images ©Shutterstock.com and ©HarperCollins*Publishers*

Every effort has been made to trace copyright holders and obtain their permission for the use of copyright material. The author and publisher will gladly receive information enabling them to rectify any error or omission in subsequent editions. All facts are correct at time of going to press.

Published by Collins
An imprint of HarperCollins*Publishers*
1 London Bridge Street
London SE1 9GF

HarperCollins*Publishers*
Macken House, 39/40 Mayor Street Upper, Dublin 1, D01 C9W8, Ireland

ISBN: 978-0-00-839993-1

First published 2020

10 9 8 7 6 5

British Library Cataloguing in Publication Data.
A CIP record of this book is available from the British Library.
Author: Alf Wilkinson
Publisher: Katie Sergeant
Project Manager: Chantal Addy
Editorial: Jill Laidlaw
Cover Design: Kevin Robbins and Sarah Duxbury
Inside Concept Design: Sarah Duxbury, Paul Oates and Ian Wrigley
Text Design and Layout: Jouve India Private Limited
Production: Karen Nulty
Printed in Great Britain by Ashford Colour Ltd

MIX
Paper | Supporting responsible forestry
FSC www.fsc.org
FSC™ C007454